Advance praise for *Faith Formation 4.0*:

This book is essential reading for contemporary church leadership. Much like a "build your own adventure" the content is organized to encourage readers concerned about evangelization and/or faith formation in a digital age, to enter the rich conversation through multiple doors. Grounded soundly in scripture, theology, history, sociology of religion, human development and learning theory, Julie describes the complex ecology of being church today.

—Lisa Kimball, PhD, Interim Associate Dean of Students, Director, Center for the Ministry of Teaching, and Professor of Christian Formation and Congregational Leadership, Virginia Theological Seminary

Biblically, theologically, historically, and technologically grounded, Lytle's ecological, media-savvy perspective anchors an approach to Christian formation and discipleship in the Digital Age that is meaningful, relevant, and—most importantly—entirely doable.

—Elizabeth Drescher, author of *Tweet If You ♥ Jesus: Practicing Church in the Digital Reformation* and co-author of *Click 2 Save: The Digital Ministry Bible*

Digital immigrant Julie Lytle has written an intimate travelogue demystifying the strange new cyber-world and presenting a living and habitable environment. She cautions us to get clear on our message, and our method, before we rush into the latest new-media trend. Faith formation comes alive in Lytle's hands.

—Eileen M. Daily, JD, PhD, Asst. Professor of Pastoral Studies, Loyola University Chicago, Institute of Pastoral Studies

How do we become Christian in the twenty-first century? Dr. Lytle offers an ecology of faith in which everything—story, relationships, and context—work together. This model provides roots for church leaders born in the digital age, wings for digital skeptics and a much-needed bridge for ministers of Christian formation.

—Day Smith Pritchartt, Executive Director, the Evangelical
Education Society of The Episcopal Church

As faith communities become more comfortable using digital media and social networking to share news within and about their congregation, there's an increasing openness to exploring technology as a way to reach beyond our church walls. *Faith Formation 4.0* connects two contemporary paradigm shifts: the rise of digital media and social networking and an increasingly diverse US population that no longer shares a common Christian narrative.

—Nancy Davidge, Editor, ECF Vital Practices

Julie brings her vast knowledge and experience in the areas of digital media and social networking to faith communities interested in addressing the challenge of faith formation and evangelization in the "post-everything" world in which we live.

—The Rt. Rev. Thomas C. Ely, Episcopal Diocese of Vermont

Faith Formation 4.0
Introducing an Ecology of Faith in a Digital Age

JULIE ANNE LYTLE

Morehouse Publishing
NEW YORK · HARRISBURG · DENVER

Unless otherwise noted, the Scripture quotations contained herein are from the New Revised Standard Version Bible, copyright © 1989 by the Division of Christian Education of the National Council of Churches of Christ in the U.S.A. Used by permission. All rights reserved.

Morehouse Publishing, 4775 Linglestown Road, Harrisburg, PA 17112

Morehouse Publishing, 445 Fifth Avenue, New York, NY 10016

Morehouse Publishing is an imprint of Church Publishing Incorporated.
www.churchpublishing.org

Cover design by Laurie Klein Westhafer
Typeset by Rose Design

Library of Congress Cataloging-in-Publication Data

A catalog record of this book is available from the Library of Congress.

ISBN-13: 978-0-8192-2831-4 (pbk.)
ISBN-13: 978-0-8192-2832-1 (ebook)

Printed in the United States of America

For Carol, with love and my deepest gratitude
and
Patricia Mumma Lytle, my mother and greatest cheerleader,
who likely was the first to order this book on Amazon—
long before the written manuscript was done.

contents

acknowledgments

Formed and fashioned by my relationships within faith communities, my beliefs and convictions—both personal and professional—have been shaped by exemplary mentors, faith-filled practitioners, and critically reflective skeptics. Mindful of the motto of one of these communities, *The Kingdom Construction Company (KCC)*, I found places "where all were welcomed, wanted, needed, appreciated, cared for, challenged, supported, and loved" and gained glimpses of the promised "Dream of God." These individuals and communities provide the foundation for my interdisciplinary exploration of "message, method and media" and my vision of "An Ecology of Faith."

I am grateful to the loving support I have been offered throughout my journey and recognize the particular contributions of Patricia Mumma Lytle and William Joseph Lytle, my parents, whose faith provided the foundation of my own and whose constant encouragement helped make this book possible; Cecilia Maureen Cromwell, IHM, catechetical mentor, whose invitation to help with the Sunday CCD program and AV resources began my catechetical apprenticeship and initiated my interdisciplinary exploration; the Reverend Joseph Vetter, communications visionary, who hired a wide-eyed newly graduated journalist and exposed me to the potential of electronic media and satellite-delivered resources; Aaron Cyrier and the KCC, my virtual umbilical cord, who introduced me to the Internet/World Wide Web and provided my first experience of a virtual community as I settled in Boston; the South Bend Monday Night group, the Boston First Friday gang, and the Cape Supper Club, my house churches, who have shared sorrows and joys, faith and life since 1987; SLAM, the Episcopal community of Saints Luke and Margaret, who introduced me to the joy of women priests and guided me as I became an Episcopalian, and St. Mary's, my current spiritual home; Peter Macaulay, my colleague, friend, and boss as I did my doctoral studies, who provided a new media sandbox within which I could test my ideas and theories and a safe harbor when fog engulfed my course; Sheryl Kujawa Holbrook and Fredrica Harris Thompsett, educators extraordinaire, whose shared vision of mutual ministry matched my deepest passion with the world's great hunger as we built a distributed learning option for lifelong learning and master's study; the EDS community, who taught me how to talk across difference; and practical theology and faith formation colleagues, particularly Eileen Daily and Lisa Kimball, whose thoughtful engagement, faithful practice, and commitment to integrating theology and culture as we equip the next generation of theological educators and pastoral leaders continually stretches my own.

Reflecting on these people and experiences shared, I find common threads: champions who invite and mentor, open-mindedness that enables dreams of the unimagined, visions that inspire and sustain, resources that are shared, and loving support that empowers emboldened action. Through them I have been formed. As they have given, so I hope to give.

preface

I am a digital immigrant. I was born in the era of black-and-white TVs with tunable antennas, rotary phones, and manual typewriters just as computers and digital technology were beginning to impact popular culture. I was in high school when Steve Jobs and Steve Wosniak introduced Apple II, the first pre-assembled, mass-produced, personal computer (1977), and in college when IBM launched the PC (1981). After graduation, I was hired by the Roman Catholic Diocese of Raleigh to help build (literally installing eight-foot satellite receiving dishes) CTNC, Catholic Telecommunications North Carolina, an affiliate of CTNA, the Catholic Telecommunications Network of America. Cable television was in its infancy, and the United States Conference of Catholic Bishops tapped satellite distribution methods to provide Roman Catholics access to religious programming and educational resources.

Obviously fascinated by technology and the ways it can be used to communicate and educate for a long time, I was open to exploration when the youth of the Kingdom Construction Company led me into the digital age. I was working as a director of youth ministries in Indiana when Mosaic (1992), the first visual interface for the World Wide Web, was introduced. This was an industry-transforming moment that made the WWW accessible to novices and non-techies. Unaware of its creation, I remember the day when Aaron demonstrated it to me as well as the overwhelming sense of connection I felt while reading stories posted by people around the globe. As I listened to the youth and saw their enthusiasm for the types of information and interaction they found online, I was hooked. Soon, the youth group had staked a plot on the digital frontier. We had a modest web presence when there were less than five hundred websites and used EcuNet, an ecumenical digital network established in 1985, to find and post information on electronic bulletin boards and for text-based interaction (early chat). With many websites devoted to Roman Catholicism, including "official" sites with church decrees and documents as well as practitioners sharing their views for the world to see, the web became an innovative addition to our senior high curriculum.

By the end of the decade, I saw the transformational potential of this interactive medium for faith formation but had more questions than answers. Academic study provided time to research educational uses of computer-mediated communication, to reflect, and to integrate my experiences with new learning. Always a practitioner first, I find that my scholarly interests develop from and support my formational and educational ministries. While focused on technological aspects of communicating the Good News (the media) as a communications specialist in North Carolina and media consultant in Indiana, I realized the message could be dramatically nuanced by the way a video camera was used. A master's of divinity degree deepened my understanding of Scripture and the traditions which grew from it (the message), but did not prepare me as well as I wanted to pass it on (the methodology). My doctorate in religion and education provided a platform to integrate the three and recognize the significance of their ordering: message, method, *then* media. These lay the foundation for this book and my life's work.

Today, I am a practical theologian, theological education media consultant, and digital evangelist. I believe that how we come to know God, discern and understand our place in creation, and choose to act on our beliefs is shaped by the relationships we have with other people and the resources they have created. Our engagement with the claims they make helps us recognize and advance our own convictions. In some instances we are leaders, in others we are followers; throughout, we are disciples learning together.

UNBINDING THE PRINTED PAGE

As I pondered the best way to organize my ideas and encourage your engagement with them, I also affirmed an awareness of how working in a digital world has influenced me and us. By their nature, each medium forms and shapes a message, as well as the sender, the receiver, and the relationships they have with one another and their environment, and even the very environment that they find themselves in. My decision about how to express my insights, particularly in a print or digital medium, impacts the way you can engage my ideas.

Consider the difference between words published in a book and the same words available online. In a book, the structure assumes a linear argument; the beginning identifies a topic to explore or a problem to solve, then the body of the text systematically presents information that leads to a conclusion at the end. As a printed medium, the text is fixed and the ideas shared through them are recorded for as long as the paper they are printed on lasts. A book is also a broadcast medium whereby a message is sent from one person to many without an ability to receive feedback. The author has the final word; readers defer to the author's authoritative position as the source of information and site of a definitive conclusion.

In contrast, the Internet is a hyperlinked, digital environment. Its structure provides users grappling with a topic or problem the means to "surf" broadly or to dig deeply through links that connect all sorts of text, audio, and video resources. The Internet is also a dynamic and interactive medium; pages can change instantaneously, local presentations can be accessed from around the world, and participants can exchange ideas and debate issues in a variety of synchronous (live) and asynchronous (recorded) ways. As a networked medium, conclusions are contextualized and democratized. Authority is shared and offers opportunities for anyone to have a voice; it is also relativized, leaving each user to draw his or her own conclusion.

The characteristics of these media—a book and the Internet (and all media for that matter)—form and shape us. In addition to spawning opportunities and imposing constraints on the ways we relate to and with one another, the characteristics of each medium influence how and what we think and feel. Some are obvious; any film aficionado can recount the effect of dramatic music and impressive camera angles. Others are subtler; news editors in every medium tell us what is important each day by what they choose to include and what they exclude (history is always written by the victors). While it is not possible to control all the elements that form and shape us, we can be more conscious of them and their effects. Thus, those responsible for lifelong faith formation need to know not only how to take advantage of the opportunities and minimize the limitations of each medium, but also how to illuminate the formational roles these media have on individuals and communities.

Not comfortable with the constraints of either the printed or digital word, this manuscript uses a hybrid format offering elements in print (book), digital (ebook), and interactive formats. The book and ebook are foundational; they systematically develop my theses that all media are formative and that faith formation best occurs when pastoral leaders select communications media and educational methods to serve their learning outcomes. Some readers will appreciate the logic of the text's chapter progression and will read them in order; others will be grateful that each chapter is a self-contained essay that can be rearranged according to their interests and needs. The website, *http://faithformation4-0.com*, stretches the boundaries of a book and points to places off the printed page that are more current, expansive, and interactive.

As much as possible, I am writing this book as a first-person narrative to initiate a dialog between us—me, the author and you, the reader whom I have imagined in your home or office contemplating ways to design faith formation options that respect and respond to digital age contexts.

The next eight chapters provide my definition of these and other terms while we explore the hows and the whys of faith formation over the past 2,000 years. Chapter 1, *Commissioned as Disciples*, explores the Great Commission as described in the Gospels and Acts of the Apostles, to highlight our call to both "proclaim the gospel" and "make Christians." Chapter 2, *Conversion and Discipleship*, relates how we live with how we share Jesus' message and invite others to actively participate within faith communities. Chapter 3, *Faith Formation and Human Communication Foundations*, explores definitions of faith formation, the evolution of communication forms from oral, written, and mass-mediated communications practices into the digital age, and the unique characteristics of each medium. Chapter 4, *Faith Formation 1.0–4.0* explores relationships between the four eras of human communication and faith formation. Chapter 5, *Contexts Matter* recognizes that everything in our environment shapes and influences the people we become. Chapter 6, *Faith Formation as an Ecology of Faith*, identifies the constellation of elements that impact faith formation and the significance of dialogue in the process. Chapter 7, *Message, Method,* then *Media*, provides a process for making decisions about the use of media and offers my proposal for inviting and forming faithful people in this digital age. Chapter 8, *Following The Way in a Digital Age*, reflects on distributed forms of evangelization, formation, and leadership.

In addition to scriptural passages offered at the beginning of each chapter that illuminate, implicitly or explicitly, the theme of the chapter, there are questions at the end to spark your self-reflection as well as spur discussion with members of your faith community. The website *http://faithformation4-0.com* is intended as a forum for us to engage one another and the larger global community as the conversation evolves—offering new insights, clarifying nuances, challenging assumptions, positing alternative conclusions, and illuminating exemplary practices. Bridging personal and communal, these media will allow the wisdom of the community to benefit the whole community. Extending the familiar adage "If you give someone a fish, she eats for a day; if you teach her to fish, she eats for a lifetime," my dream is that we can help one another reach the place where we gather to discuss fishing, share locations of favorite watering holes, and teach one another tricks of the trade.

As I share my story linking questions about God, faith, lifelong faith formation, digital media, and the impact of our contexts upon them and us, I hope you see your own story and are willing to continue the conversation online.

⇒ Introduction

> We will not hide them [stories of God's actions] from their children; we will tell to the coming generation the glorious deeds of the LORD, and his might, and the wonders that he has done. He established a decree in Jacob, and appointed a law in Israel, which he commanded our ancestors to teach to their children; that the next generation might know them, the children yet unborn, and rise up and tell them to their children, so that they should set their hope in God, and not forget the works of God, but keep his commandments. Psalm 78:4–7

My mom joins my sister and her family at church almost every Sunday. My three-year-old niece, Abby, looks forward to their weekly time together that starts on Saturday night when my sister and she talk to "Gaga" by phone to determine which service to attend: the 10 a.m. at St. Thomas More or the 11 a.m. at St. Thomas's sister chapel, St. Veronica's. This is a familiar pattern in my family. I remember countless Sunday mornings when my father would swing by my grandmother's house before heading to church for Sunday services. What is unique is that my mom lives in Pennsylvania and my sister and her family live in Rhode Island.

This routine started about a year ago when my mom lamented that her declining health prohibited her from attending Mass. Karen reminded Mom of the weekly webcasts from her church and invited Mom to join them by going to the websites of either St. Thomas

More (*http://stthomasmoreri.org/stmlive*) or St. Veronica's (*http://stthom-asmoreri.org/stvlive*). My mother had celebrated my nephew Joseph's baptism with our family using the system a year ago, so she was familiar with the practice of participating via the Internet and agreed to try it. The ritual they started that day has developed and continued almost every week since.

Because of her experience, my mom has become a digital evangelist. She is exuberant as she describes how much the service means to her both as a way to hear Scripture and reflect on God's message as well as to share that with her daughter and granddaughter. She discounts her local pastor's dismissal of "online mass" as a "facsimile" because of the real presence she experiences while sitting in front of her laptop. She describes how much she anticipates the distribution of communion that is part of this Roman Catholic service, despite her inability to physically receive the consecrated bread, because she feels connected to the body of Christ that it represents.

The service is particularly meaningful for Abby and Karen as well. Abby knows that Gaga is with them from the moment her family enters church. When she goes to the altar rail with her parents during the distribution of communion, you can tell she is looking at Gaga through the camera fixed to the choir loft. As the final song is sung and most of the congregation departs, the family moves back to the altar rail to say goodbye, first to Jesus (the cross on the altar) and then to Gaga. On the way home, Karen calls mom to share insights from the sermon. Sometimes during the week, as Karen and Abby continue their daily routine of Skyping with Gaga before dinner, stories are recalled and connected to events in their lives.

FORMING CHRISTIANS TO BE CHURCH IN THE DIGITAL AGE

Abby and her generation are growing up in a context radically different from the one that fashioned me, and likely you. Born into the digital age, their experience and understanding of church, faith, and faith formation will be influenced by a networked culture that enables interaction anywhere, anytime. Born in the mass media age and influenced by a broadcast culture, most of the decision makers in faith communities find this daunting. In addition to not knowing the difference between Facebook and YouTube, many feel ill equipped and untrained to pass on the faith they received. When asked why, even the most faithful often express a lack of knowledge about their religion and the particularities of their denominational beliefs and practices. Also, many faith community leaders often are unsure about how to design and facilitate opportunities for the next generation to experience God's loving presence, know about Jesus and his salvific acts, learn the beliefs and practices of their religion, and respond with justice-seeking action. Still, they want to be visible and relevant.

Convinced that a web presence is vital to invite those who may not be aware of what happens inside church doors as well as to prepare those who walk through them to share what they have learned with others, a majority of faith communities have added a website or some form of digital media and social networking to their communication and formation strategies.[1] Typically they tap community members with the appropriate technological skills to help—this often includes youth who otherwise may be disenfranchised from the operational side of their community. There are also plenty of books that provide instructions for how to develop effective websites to share community information and to encourage interaction through services like Facebook and Twitter. Unfortunately, most do not offer a systematic way to evaluate effectiveness and define "success" in light of the community's mission, membership, and formation goals.

While I cannot promise an approach that will work in *every* faith community, this text offers a framework to analyze a variety of contexts and the media operative in them and suggests ways to create inspiring lifelong faith formation processes that are appropriate for

---

1. Scott Thumma, Hartford Institute for Religion Research, found seven in ten U.S. congregations had a website and a "willingness to meet new challenges" in his *2010 Faith Communities Today* study of how churches, synagogues, and mosques use the Internet and other technology.

the digital age. Grounded by the dual aims of *proclaiming the gospel* (evangelization) and *making Christians* (lifelong faith formation), the framework considers how a whole environment forms and shapes us. It recognizes the role of obvious elements within a faith community like Scripture, prayer, worship, and educational practices as well as less recognizable elements like place or space, generational perspectives, personal commitment, corporate intentionality, talking across difference, and relational openness. While the impact of these is unique for each person in a community, pastoral leaders can weigh how each of these elements, along with the wider cultural context, supports or contradicts lifelong faith formation goals.

This combination of individual and communal immersion describes an *ecology of faith* operative in our communities that can be tapped to invite, inform, and cultivate faithful members as well as form and transform individual and communal lives. It recognizes that faith communities provide an environment—an ecosystem, which invites the uninitiated to engage the gospel message and forms the baptized to live as Christ's disciples. This cycle of inviting and forming occurs through the faith community's engagement with its stories and traditions, creedal statements and dogmatic beliefs, cultic expression and codified practices. Fashioned within a communal space and supported by fellow members, individuals prayerfully struggle with challenging ideas and issues and gain a vision of life greater than themselves.

Christian faith formation, then, is the means by which Jesus and his teachings will perpetuate and give direction for communal action. It unites knowing and being so that information *about* Christ and the community becomes the foundation of a way of life. By hearing the Christian message and learning communal mores, those who claim a Christian identity and embody Christian beliefs give witness to their faith in a way that ideally invites others to join them. Thus, with the gospel as source, goal, content, and process, faith communities form those who are gathered to *be church*—to become both medium and message of personal conversion and social transformation.

Theologically based in the Baptismal Covenant,[2] this ecology is grounded by the assumption that the church is not a place to go but rather a relational way of being in the world that forms and transforms us. It recognizes baptism as the time when adherents commit themselves to Christ, pledging to be the Body of Christ in the world. For Episcopalians, the promise is to continue in the apostles' teaching and fellowship, in the breaking of bread and in the prayers, to proclaim by word and example the Good News of God in Christ, to seek and serve Christ in all persons loving neighbor as yourself, to strive for justice and peace among all people, and to respect the dignity of every human being. This understanding of being a Christian requires dialogue and active participation, key characteristics of digital age technologies and vital elements for reviewing the effectiveness of evangelization and faith formation.

This book historically situates faith formation efforts showing an evolution of elements and practices that inspire a sense of identity, belonging, and meaning through four eras of human communications. Tapping the dominant communications practices of the day to form disciples and operate as the Body of Christ is something Jesus and his followers have done through four correlative eras of faith formation (1.0-4.0). The title, *Faith Formation 4.0*, acknowledges our contemporary "socially mediated" context and calls for faith communities to embrace the inherent interactive capabilities of today's new media.

Recognizing the characteristics of each medium and the opportunities and limitations they inherently present, this book establishes a framework to reflect on what is appropriate as visitors become adherents and as practitioners are formed into a way of life that reflects the vision and values Jesus offered. When viewed as an ecology of faith, it

---

2. Though the significance of baptism varies across Christian denominations (sign of new life, purification, exorcism of sin, gifts of the Spirit, initiation into the Body of Christ, etc), Christians commonly embrace baptism as a sign of identification and relationship with God (Father, Son, and Holy Spirit) and participation in Christ's life, death, and resurrection. The Episcopal articulation is at *http://www.episcopalchurch.org/page/baptismal-covenant* (accessed November 3, 2012).

draws attention to individual and community roles and responsibilities and weighs the complexities of translation across various generations with multicultural backgrounds, different learning styles, and personality preferences. It also encourages faithful openness to the correlative personal and communal transformations that will likely occur as distributive models become normative.

What follows is an interdisciplinary conversation that links an understanding of God and the stories Christians share of God's presence (theology) with how those stories shape us—individually and communally (faith formation) and the means by which we share those stories with others (communications media). Throughout, I ground theory with illustrations from personal experience. Among the myriad of questions I ask about evangelization and formation, one of my primary questions continues to be "How do we *become* Christian?" My answers reflect a personal evolution recognizing the impact of how I was formed and a series of events that changed my assumptions. As these reflections highlight, a change in context can influence the way individuals understand and practice faith.

GETTING TO THE QUESTION "HOW DO WE BECOME CHRISTIAN?"

Unlike many young people today, I cannot remember a time when I did not feel connected to a faith community. Baptized twice, I was initiated first by doctors and nurses who blessed this preemie when I was in an incubator. I was welcomed into the life of the Christian community by my extended biological and church family a few weeks later when it was clear that I would continue to jump right into life. From a very young age, I heard my parents and extended family, teachers and respected friends, tell stories of faith—from the Bible and from their lives—that captivated my imagination, motivated my action, and ignited my passion for justice. Hearing tales of Jesus' life, death, and resurrection, as well as of the communion of saints (living and dead), shaped my understanding of my role as a member of the Body of Christ. Prayerfully engaging hopes and fears, these stories gave me a vision of life greater than I could imagine, a challenge to be church in the world, and the offer of a community of support as I sought to enact the Dream of God.[3]

Within this context, my parents took their role as primary educators seriously. In addition to active participation in liturgies, parish programs, and justice activities, our home life included subscriptions to religious magazines like the *Catholic Digest* and children's television programs like *Davey and Goliath*. My mother always prepared creative ritual celebrations for birthdays, holidays, and holy days, helping us to mark the integration of sacred and secular time. I am not sure which came first, our family practices or the ritual and tradition of my family's Roman Catholic heritage; I do know that there is a significant correlation between the two.

Surrounded by an environment that connected my story with faith stories and religious traditions, I learned to embody my beliefs and practice my faith every day—in everything I did. Through full, conscious, and active participation in the Christian Story, I *became* Christian. Faith-based convictions are the ground from which and the lens through which I learned to interpret what I see and hear and touch. Discernment is the faith-guided process I have always used for making decisions and putting faith into action. At some point in my late adolescence, I realized that not everyone makes decisions this way. This insight sparked the question: *"How did I come to believe and act in this way?"* and launched my interest in how individuals are shaped by faith formation processes.

My perspective and questions broadened when I moved to the Bible Belt. After eighteen years living in a predominantly Roman Catholic context in Pennsylvania, I consciously decided to attend the University of North Carolina as much for the opportunity to experience a new culture as its academic reputation. I did not know anyone on campus when I started my freshman year, so a knock on my dorm room door during my first week was a welcome invitation to

---

3. Verna Dozier, *The Dream of God* (Cambridge, MA: Crowley Publications, 1991).

conversation with two upper-class women. Our exchange began fruit-fully as I was captivated by their infectious enthusiasm for being Tar-heels and learned about their campus involvements. I became more intrigued as they described their religious convictions. We talked for almost an hour as we shared favorite Scripture stories and reflected on how our beliefs influence our lives. I was impressed by their ability to quote Scripture by line and verse and the significance they placed on God's Word. I was also aware, though I could not name it then, that we approached and interpreted Scripture differently.

A critical turning point in the conversation—and my life—oc-curred when they asked, "When were you saved?" My quizzical look quickly communicated that I was unfamiliar with the use of this term and prompted their immediate retort, "When did you take Jesus as your Savior?" Without thinking, I answered, "I have never known a time when I did not know Jesus as my Savior. I was baptized as an infant and have always felt Jesus' presence." Their growing concern was evident in facial expressions that moved from shock to horror when they asked where I went to church and I responded that I was Roman Catholic. In the *very* brief parley that remained—as they abruptly gathered their things to leave—I learned that they identified Roman Catholics as cannibals. At that moment, I could not compre-hend what I was hearing or how these ideas could be connected.

Subsequent conversations with other Christians in the South offered an insight. Roman Catholics are rare below the Mason-Dixon line. In 1979, there were only fifty thousand Roman Catholics in the fifty thousand square miles of eastern North Carolina. Because the women who knocked on my door likely never met a Roman Catholic, their understanding of what Roman Catholics believe is left to interpretation. Friends, with whom I later shared this story, thought that it was possible that these women were taking Roman eucharistic teaching about com-munion as the real presence of Jesus' body and blood quite literally.

Implicit in this story from my first week in the Bible Belt are two very different formational processes. I grew up in a church that was grounded by Scripture. I could not quote line and verse, but

I knew the sacred stories that started with the dawn of creation, climaxed with Jesus' death and resurrection, and culminated in the early church's record of trying to live in response to Jesus' message. Renewed by the actions of the Second Vatican Council, Roman Catholic pastoral leaders revisited their understanding of Church and reclaimed an emphasis of our role as the People of God and Body of Christ. When combined with the Civil Rights Movements occurring in the late 1960s and 1970s, this meant that my interpretation of God's mission linked word and action, knowledge with responsibility. While I cannot know definitively the factors that influenced my visitors that day in 1979, their ability to quote the Bible by line and verse distinguishes a different formational focus. My impression is that *sola scriptura*—the Bible alone—oriented their beliefs and actions. My guess is that the knock on my door was their response to Jesus' Great Commission to proclaim the gospel and make Christians. Regardless, the event shifted my questions to include social formation. A lifelong quest to explore how our contexts shape us and influence our understandings, interpretations, and faith development had begun.

AN ECOLOGY OF FAITH IN A DIGITAL AGE

A lot has changed in the nearly thirty years since my explorations began. Faithful people are finding new ways to participate in and practice their faith as well as to share it. They must. Christians can no longer assume that if people come into their church structures that they will know what to do when they arrive. "The Biblical sources of terms such as 'Forbidden Fruit,' 'The writing on the wall,' 'Good Samaritan,' and 'The Promised Land' are unknown" to most of the undergraduate class of 2016.[4] Although the mix of elements to attract new members and satisfy current ones remains fairly

---

4. Since 1998, Beloit College has published an annual "cultural touchstones" list of what shapes the incoming class. It began as a way to remind faculty of "dated references" and has become a popular catalogue of changing worldviews. This phrase is number 3 on the Mindset List for the Class of 2016. *http://www.beloit.edu/mindset/2016* (accessed October 2012).

consistent—engaging worship, a good preacher, strong faith formation programs, and opportunities for fellowship—church membership continues to decline in the mainline denominations in the United States. Contexts obviously have changed and what worked in the 1950s, considered by many to be the golden age of Christian faith in the United States, is no longer sufficient.

Secular culture has shifted from generally enculturating Christian values through the middle of the last century to affirming a wider range of faith beliefs today. Additionally, some Christian parents who wanted to avoid institutional indoctrination and allow their children the freedom to make decisions for themselves decided not to baptize their children or to send them to Christian education classes. Unfamiliar with Christian language, beliefs, and practices, many adults do not know what happens within church buildings or why they should consider crossing a church threshold. These unaffiliated people are part of the growing population of "nones."

When the Pew Forum conducted the U.S. Religious Landscape survey in 2008, the fastest growing segment of the population answered "none" or "no religious preference" to open-ended questions about their religious preference. Interviewing Americans in 2012, they identified that one-fifth of all adults (eighteen and older) *and one-third of the adults eighteen to thirty* do not identify with any religion.[5] Whether based on theological, ideological, philosophical, political, or other differences, this population is made up of two groups: those who were once part of a religious community who no longer claim membership with that or any other faith community, and those who were never associated with a religion or religious practice. Some name debates about the authority of the Bible and biblical interpretation, changes in liturgical practices and worship, disillusionment with institutional leaders, or frustration with ineffective and costly institutional structures as their reason for leaving. Others

---

5. *http://www.pewforum.org/uploadedFiles/Topics/Religious_Affiliation/Unaffiliated/NonesOnTheRise-full.pdf* (accessed October 9, 2012).

have become overwhelmed by the busy-ness of life as compressed workforces and increased expectations drive those who still have a job to work harder to keep it. Family life is changing, along with secular laws and customs; faith communities now vie for individual and communal attention, especially on Sunday morning.

Embedded in these statistics that most faith communities find alarming are glimpses of hope. While there is a great deal of fluidity among the U.S. population as every major religious group is simultaneously gaining and losing adherents, more than half of the people who said that they were unaffiliated with any particular religion as a child now identify with a religious group. This suggests that many are still seeking ways to make meaning in their lives. The challenge for today's Christian is making these elements accessible, especially for those who have not grown up in a faith tradition, and ensuring common interpretation when adherents join a faith community from diverse denominational paths. This means that it is vital for us to reflect together on how we invite people into our communities and prepare them to understand and participate in communal life.

For over two thousand years, Christian methods of keeping, sharing, and adding to the stories of God's presence and Jesus' life, death, and resurrection have evolved as new communications techniques were introduced. In addition to the oral traditions passed from generation to generation proclaiming the Good News, the church has incorporated the media of the age: handwritten letters, carefully illumined texts, and mass-produced books; simple line drawings, elaborate paintings, and laser art; buildings, statues, stained glass, and mosaics; radio and television programs as well as multi-sensory electronic-enhanced worship. Today, the "rules" of engagement and social interaction have changed. Handwritten forms of interpersonal communication have been transformed by social networking, the printed page is now "turned" on the digital screens of nooks and iPads, and Skype and other forms of web conferencing are replacing telephones. Digital media and social networking offer faith communities powerful tools for passing on a faith.

In 2012, I noticed a move past the tipping point: there are a greater proportion of digital evangelists than digital skeptics. Local faith communities now assume that they need a website, and institutional leaders are integrating every form of digital resource to mark their presence in cyberspace. Some are more information oriented; others are more formation oriented.[6] Some are designed for passive engagement while others require active participation. Each is being used to ensure that every generation has heard the Christian story and has access to the means to become and be Christian.

There are a lot of elements that operate together in an ecology of faith, particularly in the digital age. One way to understand how seemingly disparate elements relate is to visualize a way to link them.

●　　●　　●

●　　●　　●

●　　●　　●

I often start a presentation about the intersection of faith formation and digital media by asking participants to connect nine dots with four straight, continuous lines. Most people find the exercise challenging. When they look at the dots, their minds automatically

---

6. A catalogue of all the digital resources available for evangelization and formation is impossible. A good search engine can identify links to suit particular needs. Some website moderators assess and "curate" resources, providing portals to exemplary practices and trustworthy authors. *Insights into Religion* at *http://religioninsights.org* includes "congregational resources and insights into religious practices;" *Faith Formation Learning Exchange* at *http://www.faithformationlearningexchange. net* catalogues current information, research, and resources for faith formation (the online and digital media section is noteworthy); and the *Center for Spiritual Resources* at *http://thecsr.org* is a self-defined "clearinghouse for enrichment programs, resources, and connections."

create a barrier using the eight external dots to create a square. Once this happens, it is impossible to conceive of a way to use only four straight lines. To successfully complete the task, one has to eliminate any preconceptions and think outside the box, literally. The mind has to be freed from assumptions and look beyond the self-imposed barriers to recognize alternatives.

In this book I provide a way to think beyond the walls that box us in to explore the whole ecology operative as we proclaim the gospel and make disciples. Along the way, I illuminate elements that include the contexts that influence the gathered community and individual members, the relationship between processes of evangelization and formation, the influence of a changing world—particularly on faith development, effective methods that recognize God's presence and share Christ's message, and the roles and challenges for those charged with passing on the faith. My goal is to ground and integrate faith formation in the digital age (4.0) with sound practices from the past (1.0, 2.0, and 3.0). Along the way, I make explicit often hidden assumptions and show new ways to reach toward the Dream of God.

☻ further reflection

- Being church moves our responsibility as Christians from going to church for Sunday services to living our faith in the world. It is an embodied conception of church. What do you need/want from your faith community so that you can be church in the world? What gifts are you able/willing to offer to your faith community to enact the Dream of God?
- In the digital age, pastoral leaders of all faiths are trying to figure out how to engage technology. Some don't know where to begin while others are moving too fast for their communities. Some are optimistic while others voice legitimate concerns about potential downsides. Where is your faith community on the spectrum between digital skeptic and digital evangelist? How comfortable are *you* in the digital age?

- Technology also brings up theological and ritual questions that will leave churches pondering for generations. Our reflections are both personal—"how will I connect with God today?" and communal—"how do we invite and welcome visitors and provide faith formation to longtime adherents?" How is the digital age impacting you and your community?

Continue the conversation online at
http://faithformation4-0.com.

→ 1

Commissioned as Disciples

> Go into all the world and proclaim the good news to the whole creation. The one who believes and is baptized will be saved, but the one who does not believe will be condemned. Mark 16: 15–16
>
> Go therefore and make disciples of all nations, baptizing them in the name of the Father and of the Son and of the Holy Spirit, and teaching them to obey everything that I have commanded you. And remember, I am with you always, until the end of the age. Matthew 28:19–20

In February 2010 Derek Sivers, self-proclaimed "entrepreneur, programmer, and avid student of life," delivered a TED Talk on "How to Start a Movement," using a three-minute video clip of a grassy hillside dotted with what appear to be groups of concertgoers. As a shirtless man dances, alone, Sivers describes the courage it takes for leaders to stand out and be ridiculed. As a second man joins the first, mirroring gestures and being embraced as an equal, Sivers highlights the underestimated significance of a movement's first follower. The first follower legitimizes the person who initially appeared crazy and becomes the catalyst for a movement. As the one who invites and encourages others to join in, the first follower shows everyone else how to participate. According to Sivers, "The first follower is what transforms a lone nut into a leader."[1]

CRAZY CHRISTIANS

In a sermon titled "We Need Some Crazy Christians," the Right Reverend Michael Curry emphasized Jesus' paradigm-shifting propositions for those gathered and watching online[2] on July 7, 2012 during The Episcopal Church's General Convention liturgy commemorating Harriett Beecher Stowe. Using Mark's account of Jesus' family fearing that Jesus had gone mad and needed restraint (Mark 3:19–27, 31–35), Curry affirmed that, "Jesus was, and is, crazy! And those who would follow him, those who would be his disciples, those who would live as and be the People of the Way, are called, summoned and challenged to be just as crazy as Jesus."

Christian Scripture is filled with stories of Jesus' "crazy" propositions. The Gospel according to Matthew starts Jesus' ministry with the Sermon on the Mount (chapters 5–7) in which Jesus describes God's dream for humanity and defines his expectations of disciples. What is unexpected is a list of those who are blessed that includes the poor in spirit, those who mourn, and the meek. This upending is reinforced later in the same gospel. Despite longstanding custom in which the eldest receives the entire family estate, the parable of the prodigal son describes a father's overwhelming generosity to his youngest who not only receives half of the estate but also a lavish party upon his return after squandering it. Correspondingly, the parable of laborers in the vineyard describes the master who pays laborers

---

1. Posted April 2010. Sivers is among the world's leading thinkers and doers who have delivered inspirational talks. *http://www.ted.com/talks/derek_sivers_how_to_start_a_movement.html*, (accessed September 2012).

2. *http://www.episcopalchurch.org/notice/general-convention-july-7-sermon-bishop-michael-curry*; *http://www.youtube.com/watch?v=abJMKeyCWoQ*

the same wages regardless of when they began work during the day. Fairness is not measured by human standards, but by God's justice.

Similar expressions of Jesus' radical requirements can be found in the other gospels and epistles. Jesus is often found in conflict with religious authorities who scrupulously follow the letter of the Law but miss the relational requirements. Unlike them, Jesus forgives sins without the required animal sacrifice and monetary payment at the temple. He heals on the Sabbath when no work is to be done. He inspires trust that God will provide and encourages communal resource-sharing. He forgives, even those who are killing him. He affirms the dignity and worth of all people and regularly associates with those who are considered sinners by a status- and class-driven social order: prostitutes, tax collectors, captives, and laborers as well as those who are poor, blind, lame, crippled, diseased, hungry, illiterate, and possessed.

By correlating one's covenantal fidelity to God with one's behavior toward others, Jesus demonstrated that belief and action must be intimately intertwined. In addition to knowing and believing, Jesus asks us to respond to God's love as he did—with other-oriented love-infused relationships and actions. He prepared his apostles and disciples through his words and actions. He wanted them not only to know and understand The Way he offered to be in relationship with God and all creation, but also the life-changing significance of following The Way and enacting the Dream of God. Jesus offered that God's kingdom is both here and now (the already, the way we find God in one another and all creation) as well as in the future (the not yet, the hereafter). This was a "crazy," mind-bending proposition for Jesus' contemporaries and continues to be so for us today.

This is a bold vision. Imagine what would happen if all of humanity changed the way we make choices and prioritized the common good over personal benefit. What would happen if we were crazy enough to love like Jesus, to give and forgive, to act justly—all in response to God's love? This is the vision Jesus tried to communicate throughout his life—and which ultimately led to his death and resurrection. It is the hope he tried to inspire as he commissioned the apostles to share his vision by inviting and forming other disciples to join them on The Way.

THE GREAT COMMISSION

The Great Commission is among the last things recorded of Jesus' time on earth in the Gospels and the Acts of the Apostles. Each account reflects the context in which it was written as the evangelists recorded what they knew and understood about Jesus and his command. Embedded in these stories is an evolution of thought over at least two generations (likely thirty to forty years) as each evangelist considered not only what must be done to pass on the faith, but also to whom the faith should be offered. Inspiring Christian missionaries, evangelists, reconcilers, and educators for over two centuries, the texts that record Jesus' commission also lay the foundation for the centrality of evangelization and formation in Christian communities.

The most well-recognized versions of the Great Commission come from the Gospels according to Mark and Matthew. In the Markan text (16:15–16), the emphasis is *proclamation* as a means to invite all of creation into the story of God's love. More information oriented, it is a way of keeping the story of God's presence alive. The Matthean text (28:19–20) emphasizes *faith formation* as it directs Jesus' disciples, and us as their descendants, to go into the world to make disciples. The Gospels of Luke and John as well as the Acts of the Apostles contain other variations of the resurrected Jesus' mandate to give witness to his life and mission. As Jesus offers his calming assurances in Luke/Acts, the disciples are reminded that they are not alone. The promise of the power of the Holy Spirit quells their fears and inspires confidence to go into regions previously unimagined. The Gospel according to John highlights how God is with us as Jesus breathes new life not only into the apostles, but the whole community. Each account includes nuances as it describes the apostles' move from fearful hiding and despair after Jesus' death to proclaiming the Good News of God's love and Christ's resurrection. These stories highlight essential elements plus contemporary evangelization and faith formation.

The Gospel According to Mark

The Great Commission passage in the Gospel according to Mark is considered by most biblical scholars to be an addition to the original author's manuscript. The brief story is set after the post-resurrection appearances to Mary Magdalene (16:1–8) and to two disciples walking into the country (16:12) and before Jesus' ascension (16:19). In it, Jesus appears to the eleven as they were sitting at a table (16:14). Their conversation begins first with Jesus' admonition of them for their lack of faith and stubbornness. He was disappointed that they did not believe those who claimed to have seen the resurrected Lord. Then, Jesus commands them to "Go into *all the world* and *proclaim the good news to the whole creation*" (16:15). The story concludes with Jesus' statement that "those who believe and are baptized will be saved" and a list of signs that will identify believers: casting out demons, speaking in new tongues, picking up snakes, drinking any deadly thing, and healing the sick (16:16–18).

Regarded as the earliest written gospel (60–70 CE), the author was likely a Gentile writing for Greek-speaking Gentile Christians. He seems to have two goals. The first is a declaration in the author's opening sentence of the intention to write what he calls a "gospel," an account of the good news about Jesus Christ, the Son of God. The second is the author's hope to elicit a faith commitment from those who hear it. Many stories in this gospel explore belief and unbelief, particularly within the community of Jesus' apostles. This account of their commissioning extends the original manuscript beyond its generally accepted conclusion at the story of Jesus' resurrection to offer an exploration of how those with weak and limited faith could lay the foundation for the future church. With its charge to "proclaim the Good News," the apostles are given the task to invite all of creation to join the story of God's love. The invitation is for all, not limited to the Jews.

From a communications perspective, the text is more *information* oriented. Many of the passages explain Jewish traditions and words that may be unfamiliar to a non-Jewish community. Like the rest of the collection of sacred stories, the gospel remembers and records the history of God's action in human lives and is a way to keep God's presence alive. It also exemplifies how those of little faith can be transformed by sharing it. In a sense, by following Jesus' command to proclaim the gospel, the apostles could claim it. For us, the imperative is to share the story. Knowing the content of our faith is one way to gain faith.

The Gospel According to Matthew

The most familiar version of the Great Commission is found in the Gospel according to Matthew (28:19–20). In contrast to the Markan text, the Matthean account does not include a call to preach the gospel or provide a record of Jesus' ascension. Unlike the other gospels and the Acts of the Apostles, there is no gift of the Holy Spirit or the power to heal and forgive. Instead, attention is focused on Jesus' directive. The apostles are told to simply *"go,"* followed by the command to *"make disciples of all the nations."* This formation-oriented mandate includes a dual imperative: to baptize and to teach. Baptism "in the name of the Father, and of the Son, and of the Holy Spirit" initiated new members into Jesus' life, death, and resurrection and marks entry into a new way of life. Taught to follow The Way, new members continued to learn *how* to love and to live lives that reflect that love.

Most scholars assert that the Matthean text was written in Greek from a Syrian location shortly after the destruction of the Jerusalem Temple (70-80 CE). The loss of the temple's identity-producing functions as God's dwelling place and the center of worship likely influenced the inclusion of Matthew's formational elements. Noted Bible scholar W. D. Davies contends that as the Pharisees of Judea rose and claimed leadership, their insistence on strict observance of the Law likely accelerated divisions between Jews who believed that Jesus was the Messiah and those who did not. Because the Matthean text does not require early followers to observe all the Law, a Jew who believed that Jesus was the Christ, the Messiah, probably wrote it for a community with Christian Jews and Christian Gentiles.

Matthew's goal was to build upon The Way that Jesus initiated so that disciples would further foster the Dream of God. The Greek text uses the verb *matheteuo,* "disciplined," instead of the noun *mathetes,* "disciple." This emphasis on "being disciplined" reminds us that Jesus offered a particular and unique way to live. His command is for the community to teach and nurture new initiates in the way of such disciplined discipleship. For us, this is a *formation-,* and ideally *transformation*-oriented approach. It recognizes that *everything* a community says and does—prayer and worship, teaching and learning, advocacy and outreach—converge to "make disciples," shape belief, and catalyze collective action. By teaching "the way that I have commanded," it calls those who claim to be disciples to practice recognizable behaviors that result in social transformation.

The Gospel According to Luke and Acts of the Apostles

In the Gospel according to Luke, Jesus first appeared to Cleopas and another disciple while they were walking on the road to Emmaus. Then, he appeared to the apostles and commissioned them in this gospel's only recorded post-resurrection visit to the apostles. The stories are linked. The eleven were gathered in Jerusalem listening to Cleopas and the other disciple's remarkable story about recognizing the risen Lord in the breaking of the bread when Jesus appeared.

The story of the apostles' commissioning starts with Jesus' greeting, "Peace be with you," and their startled and frightened response. To assure them that he was not a ghost, Jesus encouraged them to touch him and asked for something to eat. Then, reminding that his life fulfilled everything prophesized in the Hebrew Scriptures, Jesus "opened their minds to understand the scriptures," asked them to be his witnesses, telling them to preach "repentance and forgiveness" to all the nations starting in Jerusalem. The passage ends with a promise that God will provide help, which from our post-Pentecost perspective implies the coming of the Holy Spirit (Luke 24:36–49).

Like the Markan account, the Gospel according to Luke immediately concludes with Jesus' ascension into heaven. Unlike Mark, most biblical scholars agree that Luke's gospel has a sequel. Luke's author continues the account in the Acts of the Apostles where, after naming that there have been many appearances during the forty days following Jesus' death and resurrection, there is another version of the commissioning. In Acts, Jesus promised the apostles that they "will *receive power* when the Holy Spirit has come" and they will be his "witnesses in Jerusalem, in all Judea and Samaria, and to the ends of the earth" (1:6–8). The passage ends with a move to Bethany where Jesus blessed them and ascended.

The author of Luke-Acts is generally acknowledged as an educated Gentile Christian writing to a Greek-speaking audience in the latter half of the first century (60–90 CE), most likely after the destruction of the Jewish temple. The evangelist provides the purpose for his writing within the text: "to write an orderly account . . . so that you may know the truth concerning the things about which you have been instructed" (Luke 1:3–4). As evident here, these accounts teach, commission, and promise God's power. With the acknowledgement of the Judaic roots of Jesus' mission, the apostles are reminded of how Jesus fulfilled messianic promises and then commissioned them to extend that mission by witnessing and preaching "to all nations" and "all the ends of the earth." Framed this way, the author underscores that God's plan has always included the message of repentance and forgiveness for all (i.e., Gentiles) and tells the apostles to share it broadly. The Lukan promise of the Holy Spirit is fulfilled in the Acts of the Apostles after the apostles have waited forty days. Using a description of the Holy Spirit as power that is unique to Luke-Acts, the Spirit empowers the apostles to go into regions they otherwise would not have gone. This illuminates God's resolve to help them, and us, stretch beyond our comfort zone and fully embrace the universality Jesus' way.

The Gospel According to John

The last commissioning text, from the Gospel according to John, follows Jesus' appearance to Mary Magdalene and precedes the account of Thomas meeting the resurrected Lord. Beginning like Luke with a calming greeting, "Peace be with you," the short passage moves quickly to their charge: "As the Father has sent me, so I send you." Then Jesus breathed on them and said, "Receive the Holy Spirit. If you forgive the sins of any, they are forgiven them; if you retain the sins of any, they are retained" (John 20:19–23).

The Johannine Gospel is the latest of the four gospels and was likely compiled into its final form about 90–100 CE. As a work that included insights that developed over time, the original experiences and stories of those following Jesus grew into the final text, which includes more theological reflection than the gospels according to Mark, Matthew, and Luke. Most likely written by a Jewish believer in Jesus the Christ, it offers a more divinely oriented depiction of Jesus. This is evident in the description of Jesus breathing upon the apostles, which seems to parallel the Genesis account of God's breathing life into Adam.

Some biblical scholars suggest that empowering the disciples to breathe new life into the world is the author's intent. Jesus' action signals new life both as Jesus commissions and sends the apostles to forgive and as the community of believers is constituted as the church. The parallel construction of the Father sending Jesus with Jesus sending the apostles is also significant. In Greek, the author uses *pempo*—"participation"—to establish that God is in Jesus' work, rather than the more common *apostello*—"authority"—to say that Jesus' work is in God. Thus, as Jesus' obedience becomes a community norm (as the Father sent me . . .), he models what he means. We are to be with and share authority, not remotely control. When we operate in this way, the Holy Spirit is the continuation of Christ's presence in the church, breathing new life into the community as well as orienting, leading, reimagining, teaching, and comforting as we embark in God's Mission.

Each of the gospels identify in some manner Jesus' directive to invite and form disciples. They also reflect each author's context as they teach authentic traditions about Jesus and ensure that the tradition is passed on. From a Marcan perspective, "proclaiming the Good News to all creation" reveals how the apostles and disciples claim faith by knowing the community's history. "Making disciples" whose lives reflect their faith is the goal in Matthew, correlating how Jesus' life fulfilled Hebrew Scripture prophesies with how our disciplined living will bring about God's promised kin-dom. The Lucan perspective also encourages proclamation, but focuses on repentance and forgiveness. Here, the apostles are given power (literally) of the Holy Spirit as they witness to all nations. Finally, the more theologically reflective Johannine account sends the disciples with the same mandate that Jesus had from God: to walk with and breathe new life into God's people individually and collectively. Taken together, these passages unite knowing and being to illustrate how the way we live our lives can become an invitation to others. This is a story-keeping, story-sharing, and story-making process whereby community members remember and retell their experience and understanding of God's presence and the response it inspires.

STORY-KEEPING, STORY-SHARING, STORY-MAKING

Stories are important. They can entertain and educate. They can record information about cultures, time periods, and places. They can communicate understandings, meanings, and significances. They can inspire identity, purpose, and belonging. They can connect individuals and shape them as a community. They hold the memory of who we have been as well as orient and guide who we are becoming. They can cultivate a spirit of corporate responsibility. From a constructivist educator's perspective, they create our world and worldview.

For Christians, the stories of God's presence in history are the ground from which religion emerges and the means by which Christian faith continues as faith communities claim their story-keeping, story-sharing, and story-making functions. Story-keeping occurs as faithful people collect and maintain the wisdom of their tradition. This action defines and orients a community's beliefs and actions. Story-sharing communicates a vision of life with God and invites others into the Christian understanding of it. When defined by The Way, these counter-cultural actions both form disciples and invite others into discipleship. Story-making moves faith into action, putting beliefs into practice, and adding our witness to the Christian story. By interacting with and supporting one another, individuals in a faith community deepen their relationships as they prayerfully engage challenging ideas and issues, gain a vision of life greater than themselves, and go out into the world seeking to create and enact it. The result is that new members and longtime adherents are informed about, formed in, and transformed by faith primarily by their participation in it. By practicing faith, new members and longtime adherents also add to the Christian story, keeping it fresh and alive.

It is important to recognize the shift that occurs in this cycle of story-keeping, story-sharing, and story-making. The content of the stories—information about Christ and the community that follows his teachings—become the foundation of a way of being and of being transformed for future generations. By hearing the Christian message and learning communal mores, all members of the community claim a Christian identity, embody Christian beliefs, and give witness to their faith in a way that, ideally, invites others to join them. This is a relational process. Disciples share the responsibility—individually and collectively—to pass on Jesus' message. Having heard the gospel and experienced it through another's witness, new members embrace the Way—becoming church, and, in turn, sharing it with others. The gospel is not a message simply to be preached, it is a way to live and to inspire others as it is enacted; by living the message, disciples are formed by and become the media by which the gospel is heard. The medium is the message. Evangelization and formation are a circle of conversion through which faith communities proclaim the good news and make Christians.

☻ further reflection

- This chapter emphasizes The Way that Jesus offered as a means of personal conversion and social transformation. It is a bold vision. Jesus' family thought he had gone mad and many thought his ideas were crazy. It took the apostles and disciples, Jesus' first followers, to start the movement that became Christianity. Do you recognize any first followers in your community? What does it mean to follow The Way—to be a disciple (be a Christian) in your community? Are you willing/able to be a Crazy Christian?

- Each of the accounts of Jesus' commissioning in the Gospels and Acts of the Apostles provides a slightly different perspective on what is required of those who are responsible for inviting and forming disciples. How do you and/or your faith community understand this mandate?

- The most familiar passages of the Great Commission are found in the Gospels of Mark and Matthew. Mark emphasizes proclamation and evangelization while Matthew emphasizes formation and catechesis. I argue that these accounts are two sides of the same coin and both must be integrated into the life of a faith community. Does your community balance both or does one dominate? Are your community's faith formation efforts to invite and "make" disciples focused on Christ (mission centered) or making denominational members?

- The commission passages in Luke/Acts of the Apostles and John highlight the role of the Holy Spirit. In Luke/Acts, the Holy Spirit is described as a power that enables the apostles to do things they otherwise could not have imagined. In John, God's constant presence and participation is the focus as the Holy Spirit breathes new life into the apostles and into the church. What role does the Holy Spirit have for you and your community? How is the Spirit active in your community and the broader church today?

 Continue the conversation online at
http://faithformation4-0.com.

→ 2

Conversion and Discipleship

Now on that same day two of them were going to a village called Emmaus, about seven miles from Jerusalem, and talking with each other about all these things that had happened. While they were talking and discussing, Jesus himself came near and went with them, but their eyes were kept from recognizing him. And he said to them, "What are you discussing with each other while you walk along?" They stood still, looking sad. Then one of them, whose name was Cleopas, answered him, "Are you the only stranger in Jerusalem who does not know the things that have taken place there in these days?" He asked them, "What things?" They replied, "The things about Jesus of Nazareth, who was a prophet mighty in deed and word before God and all the people, and how our chief priests and leaders handed him over to be condemned to death and crucified him. But we had hoped that he was the one to redeem Israel. Yes, and besides all this, it is now the third day since these things took place. Moreover, some women of our group astounded us. They were at the tomb early this morning, and when they did not find his body there, they came back and told us that they had indeed seen a vision of angels

Continued

27

who said that he was alive. Some of those who were with us went to the tomb and found it just as the women had said; but they did not see him." Then he said to them, "Oh, how foolish you are, and how slow of heart to believe all that the prophets have declared! Was it not necessary that the Messiah should suffer these things and then enter into his glory?" Then beginning with Moses and all the prophets, he interpreted to them the things about himself in all the scriptures. As they came near the village to which they were going, he walked ahead as if he were going on. But they urged him strongly, saying, "Stay with us, because it is almost evening and the day is now nearly over." So he went in to stay with them. When he was at the table with them, he took bread, blessed and broke it, and gave it to them. Then their eyes were opened, and they recognized him; and he vanished from their sight. They said to each other, "Were not our hearts burning within us while he was talking to us on the road, while he was opening the scriptures to us?" Luke 24:13–32

Catherine and I were best friends in college. Initially meeting when I moved to her dorm in mid-semester, we decided to share a room for our sophomore and junior years. Her father helped us build a loft to get our beds off the floor and create a kitchen center complete with dishes, a toaster oven, an electric burner, and a small refrigerator. The cleared space meant our room was often the center for community gatherings and spontaneous conversations. Because Catherine grew up Presbyterian, I was a Roman Catholic, and our friends included the gamut from interdenominational Bible church practitioners to what would now be called seekers, a lot of our exchanges were about faith. As we delved into questions about Jesus and our beliefs, and shared experiences (or lack thereof) of God's presence in our lives, these conversations became a crucible that turned my thirteen years of parochial school education and a life of faithful practice into a living faith.

Sharing stories is likely the most effective way to pass on faith, particularly when we hope to inspire personal conversion and social transformation. Written slowly over time, stories are the warp and weft that become the fabric of our lives. They ground us as they record our personal and collective past and present, shape us with visions of possibilities previously unseen, and become the interpretive lenses that direct our decisions and actions. When offered to another, patterns are expanded and references are reset. Faith stories are an invitation to participate in a life greater than we can imagine.

A CIRCLE OF CONVERSION

Christianity is a faith tradition that started in and continues because of a community of believers that kept, shared, and made stories. It began as a grassroots movement when a handful of people heard Jesus speak. His words deeply touched something within them and caused them to stop what they were doing to reflect upon their experience of him and his message. Contrary to supporting the status quo, Jesus challenged their expectations and led them to see the world in a new way. This evoked not only a re-examination of personal beliefs and practices, but also corporate and societal ones. Reminded of God's covenant that lived within and beyond them, they individually and collectively recommitted their life to God and to one another—and began to challenge life-limiting practices. Their *yes* to Jesus' invitation to follow him committed them to a lifestyle that sought the common good. After Jesus' resurrection, the stories about Jesus and the vision he shared spread. More communities formed. Over time, they united to proclaim Jesus' Good News and invited others to join them, convinced that their collective words and actions would foster the promised Reign of God.

As recorded in the Christian Testament and experienced by faith community adherents since, life-transforming stories have been told and retold by disciples to initiates and fellow community members for over two thousand years. As active participants embrace Jesus' Great Commission to "make disciples of all nations" and to teach them to carry out "everything that I have commanded you," the church that Jesus inspired claims two primary tasks: to be a community that evangelizes and to be a community of forms. As an evangelizing community, disciples proclaim the gospel message through word, ritual, and action to those who have not heard Jesus' Good News. Mirroring Jesus' life-transforming example, faith-filled members ignite a "circle of conversion" that encourages the uninitiated to join them. As a forming community, seasoned believers act as mentors who guide neophytes as they learn about God's saving action. Together they discover how to live as Jesus taught, giving witness to God's love and enacting God's Dream.

Colleen Carroll coined the phrase "circle of conversion"[1] to describe the circular process whereby an individual who experiences "the radical witness of a believer living his or her faith explicitly and authentically" investigates that believer's convictions and adopts them. Having embraced faith, one in turn bears witness to others. Carroll's interest was to understand why so many young adults were claiming and reclaiming orthodox Christianity and traditional morality. One of the answers that she found was the attraction of relationships. The appeal of authentic, life-supporting, truth-telling, justice-seeking relationships is not limited to people less than thirty-five years of age.

I contend that, in addition to its invitational elements, a circle of conversion establishes the means for a community of faith to meet its dual commission of proclaiming a vision of the fullness of life and forming individuals and communities to achieve it. Re-formation and transformation occur as individuals who are different from one another and are open to really hearing one another engage in sustained critical interaction accompanied by equally intense self-reflection. This type of genuine dialogue can lead to personal and systemic change. Thus,

---

the circle of conversion is the foundation for a cycle of discipleship. It offers individuals a lifelong process to engage and practice their faith as they choose different levels of commitment and involvement within a community of faith.

A CYCLE OF DISCIPLESHIP

The cycle of discipleship can be illustrated as two axes within a circle. The circle indicates *level of affiliation*. Inside the circle are active adherents—uninitiated and initiated practitioners within a faith community; outside are those who are not affiliated either because they have not been formed by a faith community or because they were once affiliated and have become disenfranchised. The vertical axis indicates *level of involvement* from nominal, loose affiliation to formal, professional, roles while the horizontal axis indicates the *level of commitment* from lay adherents and initiated members to recognized clergy. Boundaries are porous to highlight individual freedom of movement and communal dynamism.

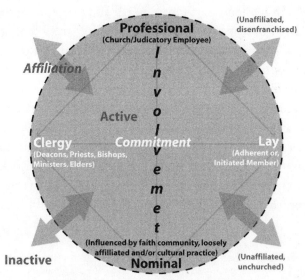

Illustration 1: Cycle of Discipleship

The cycle is designed to identify a person's current level of affiliation, commitment, and involvement within a faith community and should not be construed as a measure of faith or faithfulness.[2] It can help a faith community carefully identify the range of people who could be or are a part of their community. Effective relationship development and communication among and between these groups as represented by the double arrow lines are essential for the vitality of a community. Finally, it is important to remember that there is often fluid movement between points as personal contexts shift and individuals change their participation patterns. For example, a move, a new job, and caregiving for a family member are among the reasons someone who was once active may be less active. Ideally, pastoral leaders and community members recognize this as they live their faith and inspire one another to fulfill God's mission.

The cycle of discipleship, when viewed with an awareness of the circle of conversion, reveals a continuous (though not always sequential) process that communities of faith can use to invite, welcome, prepare, initiate, inform, form, transform, call, and empower individuals. As individuals participate in the life of a faith community—hearing the Word, learning about Jesus' Way, and coming to accept God's mission—each person's horizons generally expand, offering additional options for deeper levels of commitment and involvement. Uninterested bystanders can become disciples, seekers can be teachers, and nominal participants can increase their engagement. In this vision, communities of faith welcome people where they are and invite them to join in personal and communal activities that support and empower them to reach toward their deepest potential.

In the cycle of discipleship that links hearing Christ's message with enacting it, there are six particular groups that I want to highlight: 1)

---

2. Every system of identifying groups has inherent judgments. Identifying points on a cycle of discipleship could imply community-destroying labels. Pastoral leaders must be careful when using it so that they do not imply a label about the *faith* of an individual.

the "unchurched," who have not shown interest in religion or affiliation with a faith community; 2) seekers, interested in spiritual or
religious activities; 3) initiated, nominal members; 4) initiated, active
members living their faith in the world and/or taking lay leadership
roles within their faith communities; 5) initiated members called to
advanced study and professional commitments as lay and ordained
church leaders; and 6) the "dechurched," inactive, once-members.
Each group presents unique attributes and challenges as the community of faith seeks to maintain itself and grow.

The Unchurched

The first group, the unchurched, is generally the most elusive and
unpredictable for communities of faith. Faith community adherents can never be certain of if, when, or where they might meet
someone who has not been raised in a faith tradition. An encounter
with these potential new members could occur in one's neighborhood or office, at the grocery store or walking down the street.
Commissioned to bear witness to the gospel message, the circle
of conversion ideal assumes that disciples are "always on," always
anticipating that someone will witness their demonstration of faith
and respond to it. Thus, every word and action continuously pro-
claims the gospel message and consistently reveals faith. The hope
is that the uninitiated experience Christ's message through these
disciples, pause to consider it, feel encouraged to participate and
possibly join the disciple's community, and find life-supporting and
transforming relationships there. Under circumstances in which
community members may not know how, when, or where to find
and interact with the unchurched, the challenge for community
members is to remain steadfast in their witness.

Language and accessibility also are concerns. Words and concepts that are readily used and understood within faith communities
as part of their story-keeping process often sound foreign and are
unintelligible to those who live outside church circles. Under these

circumstances, story-sharing is not possible. The ability to translate essential elements of Christian faith into vernacular and to use tools found in popular culture are two of the most essential skills today.

Seekers

Seekers, as the name implies, are generally looking for something. When interested in spiritual or religious activities, they tend to exhibit a desire to connect with the sacred in whatever forms they can find. Sociologist Robert Wuthnow, in his book *After Heaven: Spirituality in America Since the 1950s*,[3] was one of the first to chronicle Americans' movement from practicing faith within a Christian or Jewish framework to relating to the sacred and making meaning outside the bounds of institutional norms. Often dismissed by denominational loyalists as relativists who pick and choose religious practices from a variety of faith traditions, seekers typically share a desire to understand life's meaning and to serve their neighbor; they just do so in less conventional ways.

The challenge of proclaiming the gospel to this group is demonstrating the value of practicing faith within a community context. Many seekers' claim to be "spiritual, not religious," is actually shorthand for saying they are distancing themselves from institutional structures. Disillusioned by denominational leaders' failure to practice what they preach, many people have disassociated from organized religion as stories proliferate of contemporary failures to protect their members, especially children, and financial mismanagement. In a culture that increasingly recognizes diverse contexts, multiple learning styles, and personal customization, faith traditions that emphasize multi-sensory, experiential, and sacramental forms of story-keeping and story-sharing are more alluring to seekers than those that are dogmatically based. Offering Christian tradition as an interpretive lens, rather than a measuring stick, is attractive for seekers.

---

3. Robert Wuthnow, in his book *After Heaven: Spirituality in America Since the 1950s* (Berkeley: University of California Press, 1998).

Nominal and Cultural-Practice Members

The nominal and cultural-practice members constitute a third group. It includes members who, although baptized, participate at the fringes of the faith community. Although often visible at communal worship and activities, they often participate out of cultural habit or to respond to an institutional prescription. Many times these individuals have not been introduced thoroughly to the language of religious expression or touched by life-transforming religious experiences. As a result, this group generally has not embraced the full meaning and significance of the community's stories, creeds, codes, and practices.

This population poses two challenges to the faith community as it seeks to evangelize and form them. First, although visible, they are generally not fully participating in the life of the community. Some of this population is able to identify the deficiencies of their religious education and faith formation[4]; however, many do not know or publicly express the limits of their understanding and experience. They do not know how to name what they need. The challenge is to sensitively identify these members without embarrassing them and to discern their particular, often individual, needs. Second, in addition to offering ample opportunities for multi-sensory religious experiences, the community needs to help them to interpret and make meaning from their experiences. Public opportunities for story-keeping, story-sharing, and story-making could enable reflection and provide a means for integration to occur.

Initiated, Active Members

The fourth group is the general population of committed, baptized, faithful people who have ready access to a local faith community and

---

4. For a journalistic treatment of her generation's assessment of deficiencies in religious education, see Colleen Carroll, *The New Faithful*, particularly pages 60–66. For pastoral/theological accounts, see Christopher Bellitto, *Lost and Found Catholics: Voices of Vatican II* (Cincinnati: St. Anthony Messenger Press, 1999), particularly pages 15–28 and Thomas Beaudoin, *Virtual Faith* (San Francisco: Jossey-Bass, 1998). For a sociological assessment, see Dean Hoge et al., *Young Adult Catholics* (South Bend: UND Press, 2001), particularly chapter 6.

are active within it. For them, a commitment to the community of faith means engagement in and beyond the life of the community at many levels. They make a vital connection between keeping, sharing, and making stories.

Religious educator Maria Harris offers one way to appreciate this connection in her classic book *Fashion Me A People,* in which she identifies the role of a community of faith to inspire and enact four responses: social ritual, social care, social empowerment, and social legislation. She defines social rituals as "organized actions characterized by regular, patterned, artistic movement involving groups of people banded together in reaching out." This occurs when the community gathers and is fed by Word and sacrament. Social care is both action and attitude emphasizing "relation, receptivity, and response" as members move from being gathered to offer witness. Social empowerment orients individual and communal action toward helping the oppressed to gain agency, and social legislation addresses systemic roots of injustice.[5] As such, active members remember the history of salvation and Jesus' story; ritually celebrate Jesus' life, death, and resurrection together through worship; establish a relationship with God through prayer; critically engage faith through dialog and interaction; and enact belief through justice-seeking action. This commitment to a community of faith has a price: one's energy, attention, and time.

Having embraced a way of life that influences their personal and communal choices, the witness of active members invites new participants into the community and ensures the community's continuation. The cycle of discipleship's effectiveness, however, assumes members' continued relationship with and participation within the community; it falters when consciously and unconsciously introduced

5. Maria Harris, *Fashion Me A People: Curriculum in the Church* (Louisville, KY: Westminster/ John Knox Press, 1989), 49–154.

elements distract and restrain members from their relationship with the community.

Weakened commitments may start innocently with professional travel or summer vacation, and become more extensive with increasing personal and professional demands. Many parents, guardians, and designated caregivers face the dilemma of either supporting their children's sports activities—now on Sunday mornings in many U.S. communities—or celebrating Eucharist with their faith communities. Additionally, many adults recognize the inadequacies of their religious knowledge and want to participate in lifelong faith formation, but cannot, due to the ever-expanding workday.[6] Without members' participation, the concerted efforts of community, family, school, church, religious media, and religious instruction become a "broken ecology" and reduce their transformative influence. The challenge for a community of faith is to reinforce communal relationships that nourish and cultivate faith in a manner that is sensitive to other commitments.

Those Called to Advanced Study and Professional Commitments

The fifth population has heard Jesus' call and wants to explore more thoroughly a Christian vocation as a lay or ordained professional church leader. Inspired by successive waves of church renewal within Protestant and Roman Catholic denominations, growing numbers of faithful members are actively seeking opportunities to gain a theological education and to use it to guide a faith community's spiritual growth and faith formation. For many Protestant denominations, opening the doors of ordination for women has spurred

---

6. In 2003, National Public Radio reported that the average worker had added four hundred hours per year to his or her annual work schedule in the previous decade. Assuming lunch breaks and a two-week vacation, this translates to a workday that starts at 8:30 am and ends about 6:30 pm. Add standard commute time (thirty to sixty minutes each way), household errands, and meal preparation, as well as any family responsibilities or other personal relationships, to recognize that there is little time for sleep let alone lifelong formation. *The Connection*, NPR Radio (WBUR-FM, April 20, 2003).

unprecedented numbers of new candidates.[7] Correspondingly for Roman Catholics, the wake of the Second Vatican Council spurred many lay people to formal study. Not limited by age, the call to some form of professional commitment includes older adults (baby boomers) who previously chose other professions or were discouraged from Scripture study and theological exploration. It also is constituted with younger adults (Gen X and Gen Y) who, like boomers, relish the chance to deepen their faith and to prepare for careers as lay church professionals, religiously vowed men and women, and the ordained.

Although many of those pursuing theological education seek ordination, theological shifts in the 1960s that highlight the priesthood of all believers and emphasize the baptismal call of every member have resulted in the growth of lay ministry (non-ordained church professionals) and the expansion of rosters at theological schools and seminaries. Beginning in the 1970s, most seminaries and theological education programs experienced a significant enrollment increase in their undergraduate and graduate programs. Total enrollment in theological schools grew substantially between 1972 and 1987, up approximately 60 percent when all degree programs are taken into account.[8] Currently the number of part-time students is growing much faster than that of

---

7. Although the 1853 ordination of Antoinette Brown was the first for a U.S. woman, U.S. women's ordinations were rare and were typically of a single individual. This changed mid-twentieth century when larger groups of women began to be ordained, most notably the Episcopal Philadelphia Eleven ordained in 1974. Clearly the potential for ordination led many women to seminaries for theological education. "During the twenty-year period 1973–1993, the enrollment of women in ATS schools grew from approximately 10 percent to more than 30 percent. In mainline Protestant and ecumenical schools, women constitute more than half of the student body. J. P. O'Neill and J. Grandy, "The Image of Ministry," in *Ministry Research Notes* (Princeton, NJ: Educational Testing Service, 1994).

8. Between 1987 and 1993, total enrollment grew by 14 percent. The increase in total enrollment has come mostly through the expansion of other degree programs, such as the doctor of ministry (D Min), an advanced degree for ordained clergy, and specialized master's programs for students interested in careers other than ordained ministry (e.g., youth ministry, religious education, or counseling)." Master of divinity (M Div) programs (the major program leading to ordination) have remained relatively flat since the mid-1980s. Jackson Carroll, "Seminaries and Seminarians" in *Encyclopedia of Religion and Society,* ed. William H. Swatos, Jr. (Hartford, CT: Hartford Institute for Religion Research), *hirr.hartsem.edu/ency/Seminaries.htm* (accessed on November 27, 2004).

full-time students. This steady, though not dramatic growth resulted in a 1.7 percent annual increase[9] in the full-time equivalent enrollment in theological education between 1996 and 2006.

There are three types of programs individuals generally seek: 1) personal enrichment and faith-strengthening opportunities; 2) degreed academic study (BA, MA, MDiv, DMin, etc.); and 3) professional certification and ministry formation, often in specific pastoral ministry areas such as youth ministry or chaplaincy. The financial burden of this education has become an overwhelming obstacle for many. Part-time enrollment limits some of this impact but adds the burden of work to the balancing act of school and family life. In addition to time and financial constraints that often prohibit participation, access can be a problem; theological education centers are often geographically too far away. The challenge for the community seeking to support these individuals' faith formation is to identify ways to help make advanced theological study and resources available to their members who feel called to deeper commitments. Sometimes this means encouraging active members to let go of their time-consuming leadership roles within the faith community or directing financial help and advocacy for alternative funding sources. In the digital age, it increasingly means championing creative alternatives like online and distributed learning models.

"Dechurched," Inactive Once-Members

Inactive once-members were baptized into a community of faith, but no longer practice that faith. Denominational research identifies a wide spectrum of issues that caused former members to leave. Kenneth Haugk, the executive director of Stephen Ministries who ministers to inactive Lutherans, identified thirty causes for their inactivity. Three of the most common are a lack of assimilation or connection with a community, feeling rejected by a community, and dealing with

---

9. *Fact Book on Theological Education 2006–2007*, Association of Theological Schools, 6.

a life crisis.[10] Father William McKee, CSsR, who has ministered to inactive Catholics via telephone and the Internet for over twenty-one years, identifies three primary groups of issues for inactive members: social alienation, disenfranchisement due to church doctrines and dogmas, and pastoral injustices.[11] Other issues named by Haugk and McKee include geographic reasons (unable to find a church or to develop relationships in a new church after a move), spiritual reasons (feel they are not being "fed" by poor preaching or static, uninspired liturgy), and personal choice, either due to business or disinterest.

Because inactive members typically were once active in a faith community, many should be identifiable by community members. The challenge for these communities is to establish means to develop non-threatening, personal relationships with inactive members such that the community clearly hears and recognizes the issues that prompted their departure. Having listened to what is most likely a critique of some aspect of the community's life and practice, active members must also be open to discern appropriate communal responses to promote healing and reintegration.

PARTICIPATING IN A CYCLE OF DISCIPLESHIP

As exemplified with each of these six groups, and summarized at right (Table 1), communities of faith often confront barriers that restrict their ability to fully realize their goals of inviting and fashioning people. Each of these populations presents their own set of challenges and requires something different from the faith community. Their unique

10. Farve, *http://www.thelutheran.org/9611/page30.html.*

11. The first group feel alienated and/or excluded because of racial, ethnic, and/or class distinctions, changing (or unchanging) pastoral practices in a community, or a personal or family quarrel with a church representative. Disenfranchisement typically is due to teachings on divorce/re-marriage, contraception, women's roles, or homosexuality. The third group left either because of an emotional or physical harm by a church representative (a woman told she would be excommunicated if she had a hysterectomy, or a sexually abused child) and those who needed pastoral care but experienced a minister's failure instead (a husband called for an anointing of his dying wife and was told to call back during office hours). William McKee, CSsR, provided these statistics and examples during a July 11, 2000 telephone interview. As of September 2012, his ministry has continued for twenty-one years (*http://catholicvu.com/inactive%20catholics.htm*).

characteristics require tailoring of story-keeping, story-sharing, and story-making practices so that the stories can be heard and possibly received. For example, proclaiming the gospel message to those who have not heard the Good News is challenging, especially when the audience is elusive and the language is foreign. Teaching baptized neophytes about God's saving action and supporting their efforts to live full, active, conscious, and participatory lives is impossible if they are not present. Training and supporting emerging leaders is complicated when resources are not readily available. Locating once-members and listening to the reasons for their departure, particularly when it highlights alienating

TABLE 1: The Circle of Conversion

Population	Challenge for Community of Faith
Unchurched	To identify how, when, and where to interact To interpret and make accessible in contemporary culture
Seekers	To correlate seeker's values with faith community To provide opportunities for meaningful experiences, reflection, and action
Nominal, Cultural-Practice Members	To sensitively identify who is in this population To provide opportunities for religious experiences To help members find ways to make them meaningful
Committed Initiated Members	To re-enforce and re-establish communal relationships in a manner that is sensitive to other commitments
Called to Advanced Study and Professional Church Roles	To support in transition from peer to church professional To provide financial support and advocate for new funding models To provide access to theological education resources and champion distributed learning models
Inactive Once-Members	To establish personal relationships such that the community clearly hears and recognizes the issues that prompted a departure To discern the appropriate communal response

and disenfranchising communal teachings and actions, is painful. Thus, evangelization and formation require a multifaceted approach.

Christians have always engaged multifaceted approaches to invite people to hear their stories and to deeply reflect on them. Each generation has found its own way to create transforming communities that keep, share, and make new the stories of faith that are inspired by God's dream and supported by God's love. The challenge for today, and tomorrow, is to creatively imagine how to adapt evangelization and formation efforts for new contexts and conditions.

☻ further reflection

- The story of the disciples who meet Jesus on the road to Emmaus provides an example of how evangelization and faith formation is a relational process. Using the Scripture story, what do you think are the critical elements the story highlights for passing on your faith?

- Colleen Carroll's concept of a circle of conversion assumes that the way Christians live their lives becomes a catalyst for others' conversion. This establishes a high standard for one's life. What story does your life tell? What story does your community's life tell?

- The cycle of discipleship identifies six unique populations. Each of these populations presents it's own set of challenges and requires something different from the faith community. Have you and/or your community considered these distinctions? What methods would you use to proclaim the gospel message to those who have not heard it before and are unfamiliar with religious language? How will you make the story of God's saving action available to those who are finding it challenging to be physically present? What tools do you have to support adherents' efforts to live full, active, conscious, and participatory lives?

 Continue the conversation online at http://faithformation4-0.com.

⇒ 3

Faith Formation and Human Communication Foundations

Now this is the commandment—the statutes and the ordinances—that the LORD your God charged me to teach you to observe in the land that you are about to cross into and occupy, so that you and your children and your children's children may know the LORD your God all the days of your life, and keep all his decrees and his commandments that I am commanding you, so that your days may be long. Hear therefore, O Israel, and observe them diligently, so that it may go well with you, and so that you may multiply greatly in a land flowing with milk and honey, as the LORD, the God of your ancestors, has promised you. Hear, O Israel: The LORD is our God, the LORD alone. You shall love the LORD your God with all your heart, and with all your soul, and with all your might. Keep these words that I am commanding you today in your heart. Recite them to your children and talk about them when you are at home and when you are away, when you lie down and when you rise. Bind them as a sign on your hand, fix them as an emblem on your forehead, and write them on the doorposts of your house and on your gates. Deuteronomy 6:1–9

My father is a sports enthusiast and I became one—was formed as one—almost through osmosis. For as long as I can remember, weekends included countless hours watching sports programs—especially football and baseball. Each of my siblings and I were socialized to know that Baltimore was the town to support, umpires needed glasses, conversation occurred only during commercials, and our colors changed with the seasons: black and orange in the spring for the Orioles and in the fall blue and white for the Colts (before they left town in the middle of the night), and now the Ravens' purple and gold. The highlight of each season was when my father got tickets to a game. Joined by a common allegiance, strangers united in a series of rituals—parking miles away and joining the stream wearing our colors entering the stadium, singing the national anthem, eating particular foods (things I'd never eat anywhere else), creating "the wave," chanting in unison—all to cheer our team toward victory. Together we celebrated a win, and mourned defeat. The beauty was that once I understood the pattern with one team, it was easy to correlate salient aspects with others. This was a tremendous help when I moved to Boston and joined Red Sox Nation. Sporting new colors of red and blue, I joined the throngs in exuberant celebration when we overcame the legendary eighty-six-year-old Curse of the Bambino to become national champions in 2004. . . . and I continue to support them through their cyclic highs (like the 2007 repeat) and lows (could any be worse than 2012?) because of how I was formed.

I often used this illustration when talking with families preparing to baptize their children. Typically one of the parents or godparents identified some resistance about choosing a denominational tradition for the child. The question that always came up was whether it would not be "better" to allow the child to wait until adulthood to make a decision for him- or herself. After affirming that young adults need to have an opportunity to choose whether or not and how to express their understanding and belief in God, we talked about how young people needed to learn the language of faith to make such a choice. I ask them to consider how my shift from the Orioles to the Red Sox was easier because I understood baseball and how it operated. I felt comfortable watching a game on television or going into a stadium. I knew when to stand or sit with the crowd. I comprehended the rules of the game and could interpret the hand signals and movement on the field. Without my father's introduction to the sport when I was a child, I could not have participated as fully in Boston's 2004 miracle season.

The same type of familiarity with a faith and its practices is necessary for all people—whether joining the church as infants, teens, or adults or participating as initiated members. Going into a church is often uncomfortable for those who are unfamiliar with its stories and customs. It takes time to learn and understand the rituals and symbols that enable full participation in the life of a faith community. Preparation is essential; the question is how.

Throughout Christian history, those responsible for passing on the faith have developed creative new methods to meet the needs, priorities, and interests of subsequent generations. Their educational practices reflect their assumptions about what is essential to be a Christian and live a Christian life. Jack Seymour and Donald Miller developed two helpful typologies of religious education for readily comparing and contrasting the goals and methods employed in various forms of Christian education. While typologies have limits, they are useful for communities that want to review their educational practices, identify shared and divergent assumptions, and guide decision-making in shifting contexts.

TWENTIETH-CENTURY CHRISTIAN EDUCATION

First articulated in their 1982 text *Contemporary Approaches to Religious Education* and refined in their 1990 *Theological Approaches to Christian Education,* Seymour and Miller explore the *theory and practice* of Christian education. Their goal is to correlate theological paradigms with pedagogical practices by describing how each defines five elements: the nature of *tradition* (knowledge about God), the role of the *church*, the nature of human beings (*person*), the *mission* of the church in the world, and the *method* of theology. Keeping in mind that the boundaries of each approach are somewhat fluid and rarely exclusively practiced, Seymour and Miller designate religious education efforts in one of five categories: religious instruction, community of faith, spiritual development, liberation, and interpretation.

The first, *religious instruction,* is described by Jewish education scholar Sara Little as "the process of exploring the church's tradition and self-understanding in such a way that persons can understand, assess, and therefore respond to the truth of the gospel for themselves.[1]" It is a content-centered paradigm, generally located at a school and accomplished by learners' actions of thinking, understanding, deciding, and believing. The teacher's role in creating intentional, structured opportunities for a student's engagement is crucial as he or she is the agent of the tradition and content that he or she teaches.

The goal of Seymour and Miller's second approach, *community of faith*, is to understand and embody the meaning of the people of God. They recognize that the "strategies of teaching and learning are rooted within the life and experiences of the church,"[2] and demonstrate how its customs, rituals, roles, and patterns of communicating and thinking of the church implicitly and explicitly educate. Tapping sociological and anthropological sources, this approach recognizes that communities create and maintain a culture that, as they participate in it, shapes and transforms both individuals and communities. They identify Christian educators Craig Dykstra and Charles Foster within this approach.

Framed by the developmental theories of Jean Piaget, Erik Erikson, Lawrence Kohlberg, and James Fowler, the third approach includes formal and informal activities that provide stimuli for

---

1. Jack Seymour and Donald Miller, *Theological Approaches to Christian Education* (Nashville, TN: Abingdon Press, 1990), 11–13.

2. *Ibid*, 13–14.

personal *development* in response to learner needs and interests.[3] Seeking to understand human beings, their goal has been to identify the means of attaining one's full human potential. Within Christian education, adherents design curricular processes that correlate with natural developmental stages to promote spiritual maturity.

Tied to Brazilian educator and philosopher Paulo Freire, *liberation* integrates action and reflection for critical consciousness, particularly with respect to social structures. This method highlights that knowledge is socially constructed and aims to be prophetic. Guided by our human understanding of God's vision for the world, the goal of this form of faith formation is to "help people to embody a lifestyle of Christian participation in efforts to transform and humanize the world."[4]

The meaning-making process of connecting one's faith tradition with one's life lies at the heart of the fifth approach, *interpretation*. Seymour and Miller argue that it includes "the use of imagination, story, ritual, and artistic expression, as "persons attend to the sources of knowledge, integrate them into a meaningful system, then decide and live faithfully."[5] They claim this approach is exhibited in the work of Christian religious educators Thomas Groome, James Poling, Donald Miller, and Maria Harris.

Critical of educational methods that focus on the transmission of a fixed tradition, Seymour and Miller propose an *amalgamation* of these approaches as their conclusion. Their goal is to form a partnership between education and theology such that the community is constantly interpreting and reinterpreting as well as creating and recreating itself. Recognizing that the original five approaches are generally not exclusive, they integrate elements from each with a theological eye, providing a means to acknowledge the pluralism of our time and offering a space for communities of interpretation to reach out to one another.

---

3. *Ibid*, 15–17.

4. *Ibid*, 17–18.

5. *Ibid*, 18–19.

Through this cross-fertilization, they hope that a community's mutual self-giving enables "imaginal insight"[6] through dialogical interaction such that all are transformed by their engagement.

Seymour and Miller provide an excellent overview of religious instruction, community of faith, spiritual development, liberation, interpretation, and the amalgamation approaches for the more *formal* methods faith communities use to pass on the faith. In addition to the explicit curriculum[7] designed by judicatory and/or community leaders, the whole environment and the relationships that occur within it nuance how participants receive and retain what they learn and experience. When viewed as an *ecology of faith*, the informal methods of passing on the faith are recognized and valued, the implicit curriculum is made explicit, and environmental influences are intentionally incorporated into formational practices. This requires an *expansive* understanding of formation.

FORMATION

On the face of it, formation is simply "giving-of-form." It is a dynamic process whereby elements interact within an environment to become something new. Sometimes formation occurs naturally, as when rain follows the earth's contours to erode the landscape and, over time, to create a riverbed. Other times formation is directed, as when an architect fashions and shapes materials and elements into a unique structure. Formation becomes more complex when individuals, and communities, are being formed. It is still giving-of-form; however,

---

6. *Ibid*, 257.

7. Educators identify at least five curriculum types. The "explicit or written curriculum" is a formal process typically designed by judicatory and/or community leaders to instruct and form members. The "practiced or operational curriculum" recognizes that educators interpret and adapt explicit processes. The "received curriculum" is what students actually learn and remember. The "null curriculum" is that which is not included leaving an impression that they are not important. The "hidden curricula" is covert. It refers to learning derived from the nature and structure of a faith community as well as from the behavior and attitudes of those involved in passing on the faith.

natural and intentional processes converge in an all-encompassing ecosystem that frame and orient who a person becomes—personally, socially, culturally, ethnically, economically, politically, intellectually, spiritually, religiously, and morally. How one interacts with and engages people and places, texts and rituals, attitudes and values, communal cultures and missions, each provide expanse or boundary to how one grows and develops. As such, what is available, as well as what is not available, helps direct and determine the outcome—the formation of the individual or the community. Understood in this way, formation occurs all the time. It happens in the most un-subjective, information-filled and theory-driven classes as well as immersive experiences. It flows from daily life and practice. It occurs whether we are actively or passively engaged. It takes place whether or not we are aware of it.

Tertullian (c. 155–c. 235 CE), considered by many to be the founder of Western theology, was one of the first to name the significance of formational processes for Christianity. A prolific writer and early Christian apologist from Carthage, he proclaimed, "Christians are made, not born."[8] He believed that Christianity is not something that comes naturally; it is something that occurs by living it: disciples are made. Pastoral leaders typically are attentive to their local context and create formational activities and experiences that guide and direct adherents in life-transforming ways. However, they are *often unaware of the external forces that are also shaping adherents*. Communications media are among them.

FOUR ERAS OF HUMAN COMMUNICATION

Obviously, the processes and practices that Christian communities have incorporated to proclaim the gospel and make Christians have changed over the centuries since Jesus lived, especially in the forms of human communications. *Media ecology* is a discipline that studies the correlation between the media that dominate individual and

---

8. *Apologeticus pro Christianis*, xviii.

communal discourse and the ways these media have formed and transformed the societies within which they are utilized. It is rooted in the work of Canadian educator and scholar Marshall McLuhan, American media theorist and cultural critic Neil Postman, and American cultural and religious historian, philosopher, and Jesuit priest Walter Ong.

Media ecologists have created various models for delineating significant shifts in human communications. In *The Medium Is the Massage: An Inventory of Effects,* Marshall McLuhan and Quentin Fiore claim that it is the media of the epoch that defines the essence of the society. They present four epochs: tribal era (hearing-dominant, community-based), literate era (seeing-dominant, private detachment), print era (portable text), and electronic era (sight and sound, instantaneous). Similarly communications scholar and sociologist Everett Rogers's *Communications Technology: The New Media in Society* identifies four eras based on the media functions that dominate: written, print, mass-mediated, and interactive. M. Rex Miller's *The Millennium Matrix: Reclaiming the Past, Reframing the Future of the Church* focuses on the technology: oral, print, broadcast, and digital. I emphasize media's ecological impact across four eras—oral, written, mass-mediated, and interactive, to frame this chapter's conversation about the formational aspects of each and the next chapter's discussion of their influence on faith formation.[9]

Oral Communications

Although human beings have shared thoughts and information throughout history using all of their senses—touch, taste, smell, and sight, as well as hearing—Walter Ong, S. J. holds that oral communication dominates human history (including the present). In his classic *Orality and Literacy: The Technologizing of the Word,* he notes

---

9. See Marshall McLuhan and Quentin Fiore, *The Medium Is the Massage: An Inventory of Effects* (San Francisco: HardWired, 1996); Everett Rogers, *Communications Technology: The New Media in Society* (New York: The Free Press, 1986); and M. Rex Miller, *The Millennium Matrix: Reclaiming the Past, Reframing the Future of the Church* (San Francisco: Jossey-Bass, 2004).

that "of all the many thousands of languages, possibly tens of thousands, spoken in the course of human history, only around 106 have ever been committed to writing to the degree that one can ascertain that they have produced literature, and most have never been written at all. Of the 3,000 languages spoken today, only some 78 have a literature!"[10] These statistics suggest the significance of oral story-keeping, story-sharing, and story-making.

Oral communications is the most intimate of the four forms of human communication. It assumes (requires) interaction between two or more people as stories are told and retold—kept and shared. Though story-keeping holds communal wisdom collected across time and space, it is limited by the distance story sharers travel. As people share stories, listening is as important as speaking; silent listeners can be as fully active and engaged as verbal participants. Stories are adapted to new contexts and opinions evolve through the course of a conversation. This also is a subjective process. Each individual interprets through the lens of their experience, weaving one's personal story with that of the larger community to make meaning.

Within this environment, remembering—literally and figuratively rejoining members—forms and fashions participants. Stories are the community's collected history and wisdom as well as the way an individual gains identity and claims voice as a member of a community. Stories function as both the medium and the message. What is known—what is real—is established through articulating and embodying it. As the story holder tells and becomes (embodies) the story, one learns by doing. This favors a relational apprentice/mentor model of education and formation.

Written Communications

Written forms of communication appeared about 3300 BCE as cuneiform, hieroglyphics, and alphabetic characters offered standard

---

10. Walter Ong, *Orality and Literacy: The Technologizing of the Word* (London: Routledge, 1982), 7.

signs with specific meanings—visual forms of oral speech. Using various techniques like etching stone and soft clay or writing on papyrus and later paper, the placement of these signs and letters created a permanent artifact for passing ideas and information, not only from one community to another as individuals carried these texts from one place to another, but—depending on the medium's durability—across multiple generations.

Early on, writing was limited to scribes or copyists, who typically generated only two hand-lettered manuscripts per year; written texts were rare. Still, they had a profound effect on human development. Complementing, not eliminating, the oral tradition, the written word enabled the "knower" and the "known" to be separated for the first time. Such differentiation provided a critical distance so that analysis, critique, self-examination, and introspection became possible. In freeing the mind from remembering the story, writing changed not only what was thought, but also how thought occurred. As the elasticity of oral traditions succumbed to "fixed" texts, ideas and concepts began to be represented by signs, symbols, and words in linear, sequential forms. This encouraged the development of ordered, reasonable thought and systemic categorizations of stories and information.

Over time, a more definitive sense of history developed as past and future were more clearly differentiated from the present and an individual could be understood separately from a community. Thus, rather than communal wisdom, knowledge became *personal* property and a source of power and prestige. Written forms initiated a move toward uniform messages; they also created hierarchical distinctions between the literate (educated) and the illiterate (uneducated) as well as the economically advantaged over the economically disadvantaged.

Mass-Mediated Communications

Mass-mediated communication enables mass distribution of the same message across a wider geographic area. Occurring first in print with Johannes Gutenberg's 1450 introduction of a printing press, and then via electronic media with Samuel Morse's 1835 invention of the telegraph, distribution changed from one-to-one or one-to-a-few to broadcast methods that enabled one person or group to engage the masses (one-to-many).

Egyptians had processes to print books as early as 1350 BCE, the Romans printed a daily newspaper, *Acta Diura*, on papyrus as early as 131 CE, and the Chinese used moveable type in the eleventh century. Gutenberg's unique contribution revolutionizing the industry was the systematic mechanization of the process with interchangeable parts. Portable printed text could now be distributed in larger quantities at significantly lower prices than hand-lettered texts. This launched revolutionary change in every sector of society and marked the growing separation of and distinction between the sacred and the secular.

Three centuries after the introduction of printed mass media, Samuel Morse's telegraph inaugurated the electronic mass media age on May 24, 1844 by using a series of electromagnetic dots and dashes (the Morse code) to communicate the message "What hath God wrought" between Washington, DC and Baltimore, Maryland. The first of a prolific series of electronically based technological advancements that could share sounds representing words (telegraph), actual voices (telephone, phonograph, radio), and moving images (video, television, etc.), audio communication overcame geographic barriers with Thomas Edison's 1878 invention of portable recordable cylinders and Guglielmo Marconi's 1895 space-shattering invention of wireless telegraphy (the first radio signals). Initially, military and amateur radio operators dominated the airways; radio then moved into the home and added entertainment, music, education, and news in 1919 primarily because radio manufacturers hoped to sell more radios.

The introduction of full motion visuals followed a similar route. Silent motion pictures developed in the late 1890s slowly evolved through subsequent renditions into television that was commercially introduced to the world at the 1939 New York World's Fair. Initially broadcast as black and white images across the airwaves and captured by antennae within a line of sight, television stations began to incorporate color after standards were set in 1954. In the 1950s, "cable" television was developed to enable people who could not receive air-born transmissions to get television signals through a cable. The launch of Sputnik in 1957 initiated satellite-mediated communications. It heralded revolutionary options for sending signals around the globe and blanketing a message over a much larger "footprint" of earth.

The mass distribution of printed ideas, images, and commentary at significantly reduced cost, coupled with the use of the vernacular and colloquial language, moved access to the general public and initiated what is now known as popular culture. Conversations about important events were no longer limited to the local town square and book-length discourse was no longer reserved for the privileged. A type of global awareness was initiated as broadsheets and books revealed the thoughts and words of foreign peoples. Increased opportunities to consult and compare texts launched a new era of scholarship. This shift also led to the formation of new groups, which became dominant and began to exert social, cultural, ideological, and economic influence as knowledge (not lineage or money) emerged as the basis of one's authority and power.

Electronic mass media also introduced a variety of revolutionary new characteristics. Shattering conceptions of time and space, messages became more universally available. No longer bound to someone or some transportation vehicle to physically carry a message from one location to another, electronic technologies revolutionized human communications by enabling simultaneously distributing a message "everywhere," and enabling a viewer or listener to have a sense of "being there" in the midst of the story being shared. This, in turn, encouraged a blurring of distinctions between reality and fiction (recall the impact of Orson Welles's October 31, 1939 *War of the Worlds*). Able to hear and see events as they occurred, audiences generally assumed electronic mass media newscasts were "true," failing to recognize the subjectivity of the news-gathering process and the power of news directors and commercial sponsors to define what is newsworthy. Electronic mass media can also illicit emotional responses by enhancing environmental elements with sound tracks, camera angles, and lighting, as anyone who has experienced anxiety during a horror movie, despised the villain, or fallen in love with a protagonist during a particularly romantic scene can attest. This emotion-evoking emphasis demanded that viewers experience and feel the message rather than understand and/or reflect upon it; mass media are receptive, not perceptive, media.

Although electronic media can generate a sense of global engagement, the cost of production and distribution restricts ownership and decision-making to a small circle who can direct (dictate) what is important in the public sphere. Commercial interests typically motivate content decisions, and content format promises quick fixes for complex situations in thirty-second (or less) commercials and thirty- or sixty-minute programs. Looking for the largest audiences, producers and media executives tend to choose content that speaks to the least common denominator, typically "dumbing down" a message and discouraging critical public discourse. Finally, electronic media is a "total disclosure medium" that exists to send the same information and images to all listeners and viewers—regardless of their developmental stage or ability to respond. Though programming executives attempt to establish time periods based on a particular demographic and intended audience (i.e., children's programming on Saturday morning, typically male-oriented sports during the weekend, and family oriented primetime on weekday evenings), broadcasters cannot prohibit someone for whom the program is inappropriate from receiving them.

Interactive Communications

Media scholars commonly agree that two-way interactive communication was initiated in 1876 with Alexander Graham Bell's telephone; however, the fourth age of human communications fully dawned around 1936 when Konrad Zuse created the Z1, the first freely programmable computer. He initiated the use of Boolean logic—translating information into a series of 0s and 1s that now enables data, voice, and video to be digitized and sent to anyone, anywhere, at any time. Today, more accessible interactive communications enable conversations and the exchange of ideas and information that impact participants utilizing a wide spectrum of technologies from instant messages (text) and audio conferencing (voice only) to web conferences (voice and video) and virtual worlds (representative form).

This shift from personal computing to personal communications was described in 1993 by Lorcan Dempsey as four developmental stages of the Internet: 1) a scientists' *playground* (1970s) filled with experimentation as users explored the potential for sharing data; 2) a *virtual community* consisting chiefly of computer science professionals and students (end of 1970s to 1987) who benefitted from participatory collaboration; 3) a global *academic resource* (1987 to about 1993) as information began to be stored online; and 4) a *commercial infrastructure* (1990s) as consumer interests moved online.[11] These stages have expanded to include at least two additional stages: 5) *social media,* which enables personal relationships, customizable experiences, on-demand information, and digital resources that are increasingly mobile (wireless); and 6) *virtual reality,* which allows real people to interact in computer-simulated environments.

Today's "Interactive Age" is full of promise, and the potential benefits of digital interaction are tremendous. Individuals and communities can access seemingly limitless amounts of information, and the barriers of physical distance are falling with new means to cross time and space. Still, there are constraints. Individuals exploring cyberspace often are confronted with a cacophony of resources that provide conflicting and/or contradictory information. Without an interpretive framework, guide, or community, users do not know how to discern valid and reliable sources. Tools once used to identify "authoritative" sources, like the integrity of a known publishing

---

11. Lorcan Dempsey, "Research Networks and Academic Information Services: Towards an Academic Information Infrastructure," *Journal of Information Networking* 1 (1993): 13–14.

house or an imprimatur for a book, become meaningless in a digital world where anyone can publish anything.[12] In an environment of totally free speech, digital media can foster participatory opinions and cross-cultural understanding or spread hate and destroy trust. Similarly, as digital media deconstruct social boundaries that once limited personal potential, they also can promote inappropriate disclosure and over-sharing of personal information. Additionally, there are some very significant *moral* (access, the digital divide, priority); *ethical* (behavioral norms, privacy, commercialism, virtual identities); and *financial issues* (hardware, software, training, bandwidth).

As Internet use moved beyond its original military and scientific uses, physically separated people developed more meaningful ways to interact. Early adopters created open models for sharing information, enhancing research, and improving software applications, while sysops (systems operators) emerged as mentors introducing "newbies" to new tools and coordinating interest-specific activities. Strengthened by their relationships, users collectively developed formal rules of conduct ("netiquette"), creative means to express emotions ("emoticons"), and cultic practices (online communal rituals, habits, and practices), and many user groups evolved to form online communities. Today, many websites continue the process of building communities by initiating new users and drawing them into more active participation by inviting comments and feedback. Although many of the more mutually beneficial collaborative relationships established by computer-mediated communication have been sublimated by today's more commercially oriented websites (Amazon, Trip Advisor, etc.), these are the salient features to consider when reviewing the church's use of digital media and social networking.

One interactive form whose future contributions and impact is least clear is virtual reality. Few of the general population have

---

12. In an interesting twist, the Roman Catholic Pontifical Council applied for and received a new domain: ".Catholic." Presumably, it will be used to identify "authorized" Roman Catholic sites and sources. (ICANN, *http://gtldresult.icann.org*, accessed August 30, 2012)

explored it, some are afraid of it, and the majority is unaware of it. Popularized by books like Howard Rheingold's 1991 *Virtual Reality*, and functional in science fiction accounts of Star Trek's holodeck and movies like *Tron* (1982) and *The Matrix* (1999), computer-simulated reality is primarily experimental and restricted to the realm of MIT scientists. Video games and virtual worlds are an exception. The computer-simulated environments that originated in 1978 were text-based role-playing games in which users' imaginations fueled online interaction. Today there are hundreds of 2D and 3D games as well as virtual worlds. Second Life is likely the most heavily subscribed, boasting over 31 million residents (SL's name for participants in this virtual world) in October 2012.[13] Most worlds are governed by codes of conduct, which include avoiding intolerance, harassment, assault, disclosure, indecency, and disturbing the peace. Individuals communicate through text-based interaction or audio and meet using customizable avatars or other virtual representation. These disembodied forms are a unique characteristic of virtual worlds. Though often fear-inducing since the "true" identity of a representational form is unknown, avatars are conceptually freed from societal and physical limitations of ethnicity, gender, sexual orientation, class, geography, or ability. Some are outrageous; however, many users choose to depict their idealized self or use their self-creation as an opportunity to experiment with who they would like to become. Participants also identify new freedoms without these often prejudicial markers. From the perspective of the history of human communications, virtual reality and interactive computer-simulated worlds are in their infancy. It is impossible to predict their formational outcome. My hunch is that their imagination-encouraging nature will foster creativity and stretch the boundaries of what we currently call normative. This will become more evident in the next chapter, which includes an analysis of the Anglican Cathedral of Second Life.

---

13. Total residents: 31,351,999; online residents: 53,499 on October 31, 2012, 8:30 p.m. ET. *http://gridsurvey.com/economy.php*

TABLE 2: Eras of Communication

Era	Media	Primary Characteristics	Implications
Oral	Individual story-teller	Range from one-to-one to many-to-many Personal, relational, local Hearers become part of the story; embody it Elastic—adapt to context	Prioritize memory Limited by distance a story-teller could travel Truth from story-teller
Written	Unique artifact or object—script/text, icons, paintings, stone Bibles/structures, sculpture, etc.	Separate knower—known ➡ analysis and critical reflection possible ➡ message can be shared more widely	Prioritize literacy (how to read not only text, but any object) Truth from story
Mass-Mediated Print	Printed text and images—broadsheets, books, tracts, etc.	One-to-many—controlled; same message sent to large, diverse audience Embrace vernacular, colloquial	Prioritize standardized content Truth from the printed word (the Bible) Emergence of popular culture
Electronic—Radio, TV, Film, Cable, Satellite	Electronic sight and sound broadcasts	Multi-sensory experience Dramatic Immersive	Prioritize mastery Truth from experience (that media can manipulate)
Interactive—Telephone to Digital Convergence	Bytes connect people w/ voice, video, and data	Many-to-many—open; dynamic, participatory, meaning-making Immediate and constant access to info and others	Prioritize network/participation Truth from context ➡ search for authenticity)

🙂 further reflection

- Using Seymour and Miller's typology, what model of faith formation do you think is operative in your community? What elements are evident? Absent?

- If we agree that everything is form-giving, the question is not *whether* we are forming people to understand our faith and participate in our communities, but *how* we form them both implicitly and explicitly. What factors are shaping you and your beliefs? The community that regularly gathers? Visitors? Others?

- As you reflect on your faith community with your faith community, are you constructing opportunities that are in keeping with your mission/vision and lead toward the outcomes you desire? Are you preparing participants to claim their faith and to become faithful practitioners? Are they able to see, interpret, and make meaning through the lens of faith? Are you making the implicit, explicit?

- There have been four eras of human communication: oral, written, mass mediated, and digital. Each has particular characteristics that significantly affect you and your community. Which do you find are dominant? Weaker? How does this affect communal life?

Continue the conversation online at
http://faithformation4-0.com.

→ 4

Faith Formation 1.0–4.0[1]

> When the day of Pentecost had come, they were all together in one place. And suddenly from heaven there came a sound like the rush of a violent wind, and it filled the entire house where they were sitting. Divided tongues, as of fire, appeared among them, and a tongue rested on each of them. All of them were filled with the Holy Spirit and began to speak in other languages, as the Spirit gave them ability. Now there were devout Jews from every nation under heaven living in Jerusalem. And at this sound the crowd gathered and was bewildered, because each one heard them speaking in the native language of each. Amazed and astonished, they asked, "Are not all these who are speaking Galileans? And how is it that we hear, each of us, in our own native language? Parthians, Medes, Elamites, and residents of Mesopotamia, Judea and
>
> *Continued*

---

1. A designation 1.0 and variants emerged in computer development to denote software versions. Typically the first digit represents significant enhancements: 1.0, 2.0, etc.; digits after the decimal identify minor changes: 1.0, 1.1, 1.2. Here, the first digit corresponds to a human communication era: 1.0=oral, 2.0=written, 3.0=mass-media, 4.0=interactive. A system to track technologies of faith: 2.1=letters, 2.2=biblical texts, 2.3=catacomb drawings, 2.4=icons, 2.5=fine art, 2.6=stone Bibles, etc.

Cappadocia, Pontus and Asia, Phrygia and Pamphylia, Egypt and the parts of Libya belonging to Cyrene, and visitors from Rome, both Jews and proselytes, Cretans and Arabs—in our own languages we hear them speaking about God's deeds of power." Acts 2:1–11

For the past two thousand years, Christians have been using thousands of languages to proclaim the gospel and make Christians. Originating as an oral tradition, stories of God's presence and Jesus' action in human history have been told and retold using the native tongue of people around the globe. Not limited to the spoken word, the full Bible is available in 475 dialects[2] and its stories have been translated into the languages of music, movement, and art; symbolic ritual and social action; communal expression and personal practice.

As human culture has evolved through four eras of communication, faithful people have incorporated new methods and media into their ecology of faith. In addition to oral communications, they have used written, printed mass media, electronic mass media, and interactive forms for spreading the Good News in the world as well as for faith formation within their communities. As described in the last chapter, each of these eras has had a dominant medium with inherent characteristics that affect not only the way a message is communicated (sent and received), but also create an environment that forms and shapes the population that is sending and receiving messages in it.

This chapter explores the way faith communities historically have used various media and the formative impact of each medium upon them. It assumes that media influence the way we understand

---

2. The *Scripture Language Report*, published by the United Bible Societies, uses Brazil Bible Society data to show there were records of 2,538 different languages with published biblical text: 1,240 New Testaments, 823 bible portions, and 475 full bibles at the end of 2011, *http://www.unitedbiblesocieties.org/news/1525-full-bible-now-available-in-475-languages/* (accessed October 31, 2012).

the nature of knowledge, truth, and belief, and influence the way generations of Christians formally and informally understand tradition, God, church, human beings, mission, and theology. Looking beyond the formal curricula of religious institutions, it correlates four eras of human communication to show how our methods and media shape beliefs and practices. Mindful of our past and present, we more clearly can determine future steps oriented toward enacting God's mission.

1.0 ORAL COMMUNICATION

Faith formation 1.0 recognizes the oral traditions that typically ground faith and practice in religious communities. For Christians, this oral process corresponds with Jesus' life and the early Christian community's efforts to tell and keep his story. Rooted in Judaism's oral tradition, Jesus painted a picture of the Dream of God and provided a model to enact it. Dialogue was at the heart of his ministry as Jesus invited others to join him in living The Way that God offered. With the exception of identifying a time when Jesus wrote in the sand, the Bible depicts all of Jesus' interactions with individuals and crowds as oral communications. The recorded conversations are intimate, the speeches are identity-shaping, and the message is lived through covenantal relationships—key characteristics of an oral culture.

After his death, Jesus' method of visiting communities to share the Good News continued. The Acts of the Apostles and the Epistles record countless accounts of his disciples travelling the known world to share the stories of his life, death, and resurrection and the significance of those events for humanity. Through prayer, story-sharing, feeding the hungry, caring for the widows and orphaned, clothing the naked, breaking bread, and passing the cup, the growing community moved beyond knowing the stories to become Christ for one another and the world. In so doing, the Jesus movement that later evolved into the Christian Church became part of a living tradition that maintains Jesus' presence and acts to foster the reign of God.

Today, we continue an oral tradition in continuity with the earliest Christians, but our experience of oral culture is not the same. Technologies fill our world—communications media as well as a variety of other tools, machines, and techniques—that obviously were not part of Jesus' life and his followers' experience. In addition to lacking many of Jesus' cultural referents, we have trained our minds to filter sights (homeless people warming themselves on a subway grate) and sounds (the constant buzz of electronics in our homes), reducing our ability to be attentive. The most significant difference, however, is the relationship between medium and message. To fully appreciate faith formation 1.0 methods in contemporary culture, we need to recall that oral culture does not differentiate between the story and the story-sharer. To follow Jesus' Way requires more than knowing about Jesus and God's action in our lives. We need to foster story-keeping, story-sharing, and story-making so that the Dream of God is maintained and enacted. Communal worship is one space where this can be ritually practiced.

2.0 WRITTEN COMMUNICATION

Faith formation 2.0 occurs through written engagement. In Christianity, written forms emerged about 50 to 52 CE with the letters attributed to Paul. As Paul's mission to the Gentiles expanded the geographic bounds of the Jesus movement, these letters provided Paul the ability to transcend time and space to care for his missionary outposts. In addition to leadership for the fledgling communities, Paul provided information about the Jesus movement and offered instruction and support on the whys and the ways to live as Jesus commanded.

With the continued passage of time, those who had direct and secondary contact with Jesus began to die and Jesus' return seemed less imminent. A desire to preserve the oral tradition of Jesus' life, death, resurrection, and teachings led faith community members to record their versions, likely between 70 and 110 CE. A series of subsequent redactions, gradual codification into canon, and translations into other languages resulted in the Christian Testament, which provided the early faith community and the contemporary Christian access to its origins.

Not limited to letters and scrolls, written texts expanded to include simple paintings recalling biblical stories of salvation decorating second- and third-century tomb walls. After the Edict of Milan legalized Christianity and eliminated the fear of persecution, Christian art shifted from personal artifacts with symbolic meaning in hidden spaces to include explicit public religious expression integrated into the cultural framework. Icons offered windows to heaven, symbolic truths, and spiritual ideals and magnificently adorned basilicas emerged in the ancient skyline. These "stone Bibles" proclaimed the Word through stained glass, frescos, mosaics, and statues, and provided the illiterate a means to "read" stories of faith. Particularly between the seventh and thirteenth centuries, beautifully hand-lettered and illumined manuscripts were created both to serve as an act of worship for the illuminator and to ensure that the gospel passed from one generation to the next, especially among the literate.

Written communications enabled the separation of the knower from the known. As subsequent generations reflected on Jesus' message and recorded their convictions, Christianity expanded from instructions for Christian living based on The Way to incorporate systemic thought. Compendiums of written documents reveal the evolution of theological discourse as church leaders started asking questions about God and God's being, defining Christian beliefs, and codifying Christian practices. Challenges about authority and interpretation led to official written pronouncements, delineating what was and was not within bounds.

Over time, other formulations of the Christian tradition emerged, attempting both to provide schemas for proper interpretation (i.e., Scripture, tradition, reason, and personal experience) and to standardize ritual practices and meaning-making. This ensured a sense of continuity in form and function across Christian communities. These codifications also ensured that the community literally re-membered Christ and figuratively made him present through that recollection. Thus, written records provide access through time and continuity across space so that current adherents can interact with the earliest Christians as well as subsequent generations. They define boundaries and can be used as an interpretive lens when discerning truth. One challenge for the present posed by this era's written environment highlights different understandings of time. Scribes spent hours prayerfully considering God's Word while producing illuminated texts, and the literate both patiently waited to receive them and made space to read them aloud and digest their meaning. Contemporary culture's need for immediacy restricts many people's ability to fully interact with our preserved texts and the insights they offer.

3.0 MASS-MEDIATED COMMUNICATION

Faith formation 3.0 is known for mass distribution of the same message across a wider geographic area than previously conceived. This led to the emergence of popular culture and spurred great debate as previously disparate places gained access to one another's thoughts, beliefs, and practices. The era began with the innovation of Gutenberg's press and launch of the Protestant Revolution, which shared a symbiotic relationship as sociologist and feminist educator Carmen Luke successfully argues in *Pedagogy, Printing, and Protestantism*.[3] Even though the European printing press produced its first book in 1450 and after fifty years some thirty thousand to fifty thousand editions had been produced, printed technology did not make an impact until after Luther posted his ninety-five theses on the doors of Wittenberg castle church and some reform-minded activists decided to publish them. Luther's intent was to initiate an academic dialogue among a small group of scholars; instead, his theses were distributed throughout Europe within two weeks.

---

3. Carmen Luke, *Pedagogy, Printing, and Protestantism* (New York: SUNY Press, 1989).

Luther's encouragement to use the vernacular and make Scripture widely available helped create an environment that enabled both laity and scholars to examine Scripture with individual scrutiny. Once limited to the libraries of the wealthy, personal copies of the Bible were more readily available. Print technology also permitted reformers to work out how the teaching contained in Scripture could be made ever present. Thus, in addition to the availability of an economical means to reproduce vast quantities of the Bible and reformation literature, Gutenberg's invention gained its niche through the union of three elements: radical reformers' desire to put their message and the Word in every home; missionaries' eagerness to educate the general population so that they could read and interpret the Scriptures for themselves; and a large, geographically dispersed population's interest in gaining access to this information.

Printed mass media initiated discourses on religious, social, and political thought and expanded participation throughout Germany, and later Europe and the rest of the known world. The combination of a new communicative technology with reformers' challenges of contemporary assumptions catapulted local conversations into national, continental, and even intercontinental concerns as vernacular Bibles, sermons, treatises, and tracts on topics ranging from the new understandings of the faith to family relations and childrearing proliferated. Paradigm shifts resulted as revolutionary ideas infiltrated contemporary life. Within Christianity, these shifts included focus upon "the Word," challenges to the Roman Catholic Church's authority, and schisms from Roman ecclesial structures. In response, counter-reform movements also embraced these technologies to regain/maintain control by standardizing theological concepts and ritual practices, emphasizing a unified message, and reinstating the Church as the proper authority. Sweeping shifts continued as the printed mass media revolution evolved into an electronic one.

The early history of the relationship between religious communities and electronic mass media producers can be viewed positively as pastoral leaders experimented with new ways to proclaim the gospel and make Christians. The first Christian appropriation of electronic mass media occurred when the first broadcast radio station, Pittsburgh's KDKA, went "on air." Convinced that the sounds of his faith community should be shared with the country, a Westinghouse engineer who sang in his church choir helped Calvary Episcopal Church's Sunday evening prayer service become the first American religious broadcast in 1921. Though acceptance of religious broadcasts was mixed, some claiming that it was a sinful frivolity, "many saw radio as a way to reach, enlighten, and possibly convert an audience far larger than any church, tabernacle, or revival tent could ever accommodate."[4] The Department of Commerce allocated a wavelength (83.3 kilocycles) for religious programming and established government support for religious broadcast development while pioneers like Aimee Semple McPherson and Paul Rader built radio stations to broadcast church services, Morning Prayer, inspirational talk shows, and entertainment-oriented programs. By 1925, sixty-three religious organizations held radio licenses and the Federation of Churches (mainstream Protestant, Roman Catholic, and Jewish) gained assurance that they would receive free or sustaining network time when NBC debuted as a coast-to-coast network in 1927. Soon listeners could hear intelligent, balanced representations of the nation's three major religious groups through radio programs like NBC's *National Radio Pulpit, Catholic Hour,* and *Message of Israel.*

As television was introduced in the United States, mainline churches were experiencing the peak of their membership and influence, so collaboration continued. Mainline faith groups were provided free, sustaining airtime to distribute informational and inspirational programs as an extension of the church or synagogue, as well as to broadcast worship services on high holidays like Easter and Christmas. This frustrated more conservative religious groups who felt "squeezed out" of radio and television by their more liberal

4. Hal Erickson, *Religious Radio and Television in the United States, 1921-1991: The Programs and Personalities* (Jefferson, NC: McFarland & Company, Inc., 1992), 2.

counterparts. The resulting battle for access to airspace fundamentally shifted the landscape not only for television but also radio when these churches began paying for airtime.[5]

Televangelists dominated the airwaves from the mid-1950s onward and narrowed the definition of religion for the general public. The electronic church maintained two or three well-chosen, entertainment-oriented formats that included a weekly revival or religious service, a talk show, and/or a news magazine. These programs generally focused on several core themes: the inevitability of sin, the need to be spiritually born-again, individual salvation, rejection of the world, Jesus' divinity, the importance of the Bible, one's tasks as a Bible-believer, and the mandate to spread the gospel. They also created intimacy at a distance, developing what viewers perceived as a one-on-one relationship with the host. They accomplished this by combining charismatic personalities, conversational style, personalized rhetoric, comfortable set designs, and subjective camera techniques. These productions contributed to a considerable reconfiguration of the U.S. sociopolitical landscape through the 1980s that included a resurgence of the Christian Right, the meteoric rise of televangelism, and popular culture's embrace of fundamentalist ideals.

Mass mediate forms of evangelization and formation were not restricted to radio and television. Since the late 1970s, religious communicators have also taken advantage of satellite technology to reach national and international audiences. The Christian Broadcast Network, now called the Family Channel, was the first religious service, and second broadcast network, to utilize satellite technology. An outgrowth of Pat Robertson's early efforts in local radio and television broadcasting, CBN was carried by six thousand cable systems, making it the fifth-largest cable service in 1986. After initially appearing on CBN, Mother Angelica established the first national Catholic cable television presence in 1981 with her

---

5. In 1957, 47 percent of religious broadcasts were paid; by 1978, 92 percent of inspirational programming was!

twenty-four-hour-a-day Alabama-based Eternal Word Television Network (EWTN).

Although initially popular as a means to diversify a cable system's line-up, religious programming began to lose its appeal in the mid- to late-1980s in response to some of the televangelism scandals. Rather than lose airspace, a group of cable operators and religious broadcasters formed the National Interfaith Cable Coalition, Inc. and created Vision Interfaith Satellite Network. With strict rules regarding fund solicitation and content, VISN proved to be an apt alternative for cable networks. Unfortunately, although initially well received, continued corporate mergers led to limited programming presence today.[6]

Finally, not all religious programming was designed for entertainment-oriented distribution outlets. Recognizing the benefits of extended reach, many denominations began exploring intra-church communications practices via satellite. The National Conference of Catholic Bishops (NCCB) established the Catholic Telecommunications Network of America (CTNA) in 1981 and distributed video programming for internal church use as well as cable distribution to the homes. Until it was dissolved in July 1995, CTNA served the church in five broad ways: electronic mail; teleconferencing on a variety of topics; transmission of photos and news for the Catholic News Service; special programming for schools, hospital, and parish personnel; and programming for home audiences. Similarly, the Southern Baptist Conference, through its Radio and Television Commission, established ACTS (American Christian Television Service) and Baptist TelNet, while the Church of Christ of Latter Day Saints began installing downlinks at congregational centers. Also, Tony Verna linked over 1.5 million people in seventeen countries on five continents with twenty-four satellites and thirty transponders for an hour-long "Prayer for the World" as a one-time, ecumenical event on June 6, 1987. While these outlets creatively utilized satellite technology, they failed to establish a sustainable model of existence.

---

6. First VISN, then VISN/ACTS, then the Family and Values Network, then the Hallmark Channel in 2001when the Jim Henson Company bought it; they then limited the spiritually oriented programs.

This survey of radio, television, cable, and satellite-delivery efforts suggest the breadth and creativity of these electronically mass-mediated efforts and provide many life-affirming characteristics. From an institutional perspective, these technologies assure standardization and uniformity as the same message is conveyed to a very large audience. From a personal perspective, individuals could learn about faith traditions and religious practices in the comfort of their homes before attending a service, and gain inspiration from theatrically produced inspirational stories. Unfortunately, there are life-diminishing communicative characteristics as well. Standardization can encourage conformity and lead to rigidity. As a *passive* medium, radio and video broadcasts lack opportunities for direct engagement and dialogical interaction with other readers or audience members, as well as with the producers, writers, actors, sponsors, etc. Additionally, from a production and distribution perspective, mass media typically restrict message-related decisions to an authoritative individual or body, narrowing the perspectives presented and voices heard. Generally reinforcing hierarchical structures and the dominant culture, counter-cultural information and alternative views are usually absent. Finally, the expense of creating and distributing programs and broadcast's cult of personality ethos has left many producers precariously balancing focus on God with focus on fundraising and/or a celebrity.

4.0 INTERACTIVE MEDIA

Formation 4.0 is inherently interactive, giving individuals not only the ability to *receive* communication but also to *respond*. By converting voice, video, and data into digital signals, people and resources can be connected (almost) anywhere and at (almost) any time. Although these multi-directional, multi-modal capabilities were available when networked computing was introduced, until recently these characteristics have been underutilized, especially by faith communities. Paralleling the shift from personal computing to personal communications and social networking, churches initially used computer technology for desktop publishing, including church bulletins and event promotions as well as data management such as membership rolls, pledge tracking, church budgets, and the like. With technological advances that enabled computers to communicate, Christians began to explore digitally mediated relationships and evaluate the computer's usefulness for ministerial purposes.

The earliest forms of computer-mediated communication (CMC) occurred as individual Christians attached modems to their personal computers to reach one another through text-based bulletin boards, special interest groups, Christian conferences, and user groups. The United Methodists were first on what is now the Internet, testing the water in 1983 by distributing an electronic newsletter before using the networks to share daily news stories, commentaries, and news briefs from their 1984 General Convention. Similar pilot projects between 1984 and 1986—some with direct ecclesial ties, others more informal—spawned a variety of denominationally linked user groups and practical resource development. Informal collaborations produced very popular weekly sermon helps—*The Lectionary* and *Sermonshop,* a weekly computer magazine—*The Monday Night Connection,* and live chat conferences. These led to the creation of an Interfaith Center, which formally incorporated as Ecunet in 1986.

Ecunet's early interactive efforts generated enthusiasm about CMC's ability to transcend time and space; however, formational and transformational aspects were unclear until the January 28, 1986 shuttle Challenger disaster when this ecumenical group likely offered the first virtual worship service. Though text-based, the memorial service[7] led by four pastors from different denominations provided space for an international gathering to post prayers and thoughts about the tragedy. The "coffee hour" at a virtual speakeasy after the service enabled people to express their sadness about the explosion. David Lochhead, one of the first theologians to enter cyberspace and an Ecunet founder, described how the service catalyzed a profound

---

7. The service bulletin is at *http://www.glaird.com/uchg1011.htm* (accessed October 31, 2012).

energy between people from Hawaii to Nova Scotia as together they prayed and mourned the loss of the crew.[8]

The presence of faith-related sites on the web consistently grew in the late 1980s and 1990s, however the majority functioned like broadcast media. Despite a lack of interpersonal interaction, many offered creative ways to engage information, like the American Bible Society's online multimedia translation of Jesus' Parable of the Good Samaritan that included Scripture texts, archeological information, maps, games, and a video stream.[9] There are notable exceptions. Faith groups were well represented as Usenet groups continued to expand, add interactive newsgroups and chat rooms for topical discussions, recreational activities, news sharing, and community organizing. Roman Catholic Archbishop Jacques Gaillot created the first virtual diocese (*http://www.partenia.org*) after he was abruptly removed from his position as bishop of Evreux in January 1995. He offers pastoral care to "the excluded" in seven languages (French, English, German, Italian, Spanish, Portuguese, and Dutch) and calls parishioners spanning the planet to act with justice. Online communities emerged with the support of publishing houses including Loyola Press's FindingGod.com, Sadlier's CyberFaith.com, RCL's WholeCommunityCatechesis.com, and Saint Anthony Messenger Press's AmericanCatholic.org.

The beginning of the twenty-first century marked a technological move to web 2.0 in 2004 and a corresponding social turn toward improved applications of relationship-cultivating interactive media. Americans quickly and creatively responded to the rapid introductions of social media applications including blogs (1999), smartphones (Palm Kyocera 6035, first in U.S.) (2001), Wikipedia (2001), MySpace (2003), Second Life (2003), Skype (2003), Facebook

---

8. From August 30, 1995, email with DAN.parti@ecunet.org recounting Ecunet history.

9. In the 1990s, the American Bible Society produced The New Media Bible and considered it a new translation, not an interpretation. See Paul Soukup, S.J. and Robert Hodgson, ed. *Fidelity and Translation: Communicating the Bible in New Media* (Franklin, WI: Sheed & Ward, 1999) and *From One Medium to Another: Communicating the Bible through Multimedia* (Kansas City, MO: Sheed & Ward, 1997). Previously available at *http://www.newmediabible.org*, this URL now directs users to the Campus Crusade for Christ's "The Jesus Film Project" (accessed October 31, 2012).

(2004), World of Warcraft (2004), YouTube (2005), RSS (Real Simple Syndication) (2005), Macromedia Breeze live web conferencing (2005), and Twitter (2006). Faith communities are slowly responding by blending new resources to reach the unaffiliated as well as engage and support faith community members. The 2004 Pew Internet and American Life Project Report, *Faith Online*,[10] identified nearly 82 million Americans—64 percent of Internet users—perform spiritual and religious activities online to supplement their ties to traditional institutions. More recently, the 2010 Hartford Institute for Religion Research national survey of 11,077 of the nation's 335,000 congregations found that 69 percent have websites (up from 33 percent ten years previous), 4 percent have Facebook pages, and 1 percent stream worship[11] services.[12] Pastoral leaders are increasingly using blogs, Twitter, and other interactive forums to share information, present ideas, and initiate genuine dialogue. Even Pope Benedict XVI has been an unexpectedly strong supporter of social media, having launched a YouTube channel with six languages in 2008 as well as a Facebook and iPad app, "Pope2you," in 2009,[13] and encouraging priests to proclaim the gospel by blogging and using new web communications tools.

---

10. *http://pewinternet.org/Reports/2004/Faith-Online.aspx* (accessed October 31, 2012).

11. A U.S. copyright law religious service exemption allows churches to perform/display certain copyrighted works in services without permission or royalty, but not retransmit. A presenter's permission may make a sermon or other pastoral message possible, however music and other creative expressions are likely copyright protected. WORSHIPcast and Christian Copyright Solutions are two who are collaborating with ASCAP, BMI, and SESAC to prevent infringement *http://www.copyrightcommunity.com* (accessed October 31, 2012).

12. Scott Thumma, "Virtually Religious: Technology and Internet Use in American Congregations." *Faith Communities Today 2010 (FACT)*, Hartford Institute for Religion Research, March 7, 2012. *http://faithcommunitiestoday.org/report-congregations-and-their-use-internet-technologies*

13. "Priests can rightly be expected to be present in the world of digital communications as faithful witnesses to the Gospel, exercising their proper role as leaders of communities which increasingly express themselves with the different 'voices' provided by the digital marketplace. Priests are thus challenged to proclaim the Gospel by employing the latest generation of audiovisual resources (images, videos, animated features, blogs, websites) which, alongside traditional means, can open up broad new vistas for dialogue, evangelization and catechesis." Pope Benedict XVI 44th World Communication Day, May 16, 2010, *http://www.vatican.va/holy_father/benedict_xvi/messages/communications/documents/hf_ben-xvi_mes_20100124_44th-world-communications-day_en.html*

With rosters dwindling, many faith communities have designed evangelism-oriented sites to reach the growing population of "nones." OnceCatholic.org and ReThinkChurch.org illustrate sites designed to encourage asynchronous interaction between denominational representatives and the unaffiliated. Launched in 2001, OnceCatholic was likely the first interactive site designed to enable those who left the Roman Catholic Church to interact with companions in hope of healing hurts and encouraging former members to "come home." Similarly, the United Methodist Church's campaign to ReThink Church, launched in 2009, uses threaded discussions to help individuals and communities focus on church as a way of life. The site hosts "conversations," encouraging viewers to "share what is on your mind," and identifies ways to meet others and get involved in activities that will change the world.

Faithful people and church professionals continue to develop new faith formation resources designed to support new initiates and active members. Luther Seminary Associate Professor Mary Hess spearheaded the creation of FeAutor.org as a place for pastoral leaders to share religious resources using Creative Commons licenses.[14] The Reverend Thomas Brackett, Episcopal Church planting and ministry redevelopment officer, is using live web conferencing to gather and support ministry innovators, church planters, and ministry redevelopers as well as to provide coaching and consulting sessions to ministry leaders. Lifelong learning and theological education is more readily available through distributed models. The Association of Theological Schools lists over 135 member schools with distance learning options for certificates and degrees, and other faith-based institutions are providing free and affordable interactive workshops, web conferences, and courses like Gordon-Conwell's "Dimensions of Faith" (*http://my.gordonconwell.edu/dimensions*), the University of Notre Dame's Satellite Theological Education Program (STEP) (*http://step.nd.ed*), Education for Ministry Online (*http://www.*

14. Creative Commons are copyright licenses designed to protect intellectual property and give credit for work while simplifying the process for sharing creative works. *http://www.creativecommons.org*

sewanee.edu/EFM/EFMONLINE.htm), and the Transformingth-eChurch.org. Additionally, mobile technologies now enable most of these resources to be available anywhere and anytime.

As faith communities gain comfort with digital technologies that expand their ability to connect with one another, the creation of virtual churches is raising the most questions and concerns. Unable to presume that a physically gathered community will remain the norm for faith communities, some early adopters are exploring the potential of online communities. Some virtual churches are designed to complement brick-and-mortar faith communities like Fort Lauderdale's Sunshine Cathedral, which gathers regularly at 1480 SW 9th Avenue and at Sunshine Cathedral of Second Life (*http://secondlife.sunshinecathedral.org*), while others are online-only like the Anglican Cathedral of Second Life (*http://slangcath.wordpress.com*) and Faith Village (*http://www.faithvillage.com*). Taking advantage of a multi-directional, multi-sensory environment, the sponsors of these virtual spaces are creating immersive worlds so that individuals will always have a space to gather to share stories of God's presence, hear God's call, and engage God's mission. They also offer support to those who, for whatever reason, are not entering a physical church or want to supplement their real-world commitments with virtual ones. They are convinced that virtual churches are a natural evolution of ways to respond to Jesus' command to proclaim the gospel to all the nations. Their efforts are challenging faith communities in real life and cyberspace to reconsider the boundaries of Christian life in each.

Faith formation 4.0 is still in its infancy even though the technological innovations that initiated it were introduced as early as 1876 when Alexander Graham Bell invented the telephone. Three primary characteristics frame this era: 1) a convergence of voice, video, and data on one digital platform; 2) ubiquitous access—anywhere, anytime, by anyone with network connectivity; and 3) the potential for multipoint interactivity—with seemingly endless combinations of sending and receiving messages from one-to-one to many-to-many. Secondary characteristics include a democratization of authorship, easy replication, personalization, and customization. Paralleling paradigm shifts in contemporary culture, these characteristics are initiating evolutionary and revolutionary changes in faith communities. Religious institutions and faithful people are still trying to learn the language of these technologies and use them appropriately to invite seekers and support longtime members.

Digital media and social networking are easier to create and update, less expensive to produce, and more broadly accessible than previous media. This means faith communities can tailor websites and networked resources to meet the needs of particular groups along the cycle of discipleship. Although networked computers were initially viewed with skepticism as disembodying and isolating technologies, the growing awareness of social media's ability to convey social presence—particularly when the alternative is no pastoral presence—is changing attitudes and increasing use for everything from pastoral care to lifelong learning.

Typically fostering a distributive network, the resulting collaborative leadership and flattened authority are being both celebrated and lamented as grassroots movements gain voice (and power) and institutional authorities lose control. Notions of time and space are also shifting as interactive media leave impressions that we are always available and the borders between public and private are blurring. Overwhelmed by the breadth of information and resources, seekers as well as longtime members would benefit from mentors who can guide them through the maze to recognize appropriate resources. The concept of virtual churches and dispersed participants is challenging central assumptions about what it means to be church and whether or not physical structures need to be maintained. Openness to the possibilities of experiencing God's presence remains central to the efficacy of digital media and social networking for personal conversion and social transformation.

😊 further reflection

- With the exception of the apostles and disciples who lived and walked with Jesus during his lifetime, all of Jesus' followers have come to know him through some mediated form. How have you experienced mediated faith?

- Each of the four eras of human communication—oral, written, mass mediated, and digital—has significantly affected our efforts to proclaim the gospel and make Christians. Can you identify ways in which your community includes elements from each era and their impact on your community?

- Previous eras of human communication lasted long enough for the majority of the population to be formed by the same dominant medium. Today's rapid introduction of new communications technologies means that each of the four dominant communications streams has formed a segment of the population. What are the dominant media that have formed members of your community? How are you integrating different technological languages to reach them?

- The interactive age offers opportunities to connect anytime, anywhere, for informational, formational, and transformational results? Have you used the Internet or social media to get information about your religion, practice your faith (prayer, mediation, spiritual direction, etc.), or engage in conversations with others about faith? Do you believe there are media that can convey enough social presence to establish new meaningful relationships? Sustain pre-existing ones?

- The emergence of virtual churches, replicating many forms of "real life," is challenging conceptions of what is church. What do you think are the strengths and limitations of virtual churches? What impact may they have on community life? Worship? Sacraments? Evangelization? Faith formation?

Continue the conversation online at
http://faithformation4-0.com.

⇒ 5

Contexts Matter

> They came to Bethsaida. Some people brought a blind man to him and begged him to touch him. He took the blind man by the hand and led him out of the village; and when he had put saliva on his eyes and laid his hands on him, he asked him, "Can you see anything?" And the man looked up and said, "I can see people, but they look like trees, walking." Then Jesus laid his hands on his eyes again; and he looked intently and his sight was restored, and he saw everything clearly. Then he sent him away to his home, saying, "Do not even go into the village." Mark 8:22–26

Growing up in Pennsylvania barely fifteen miles from the Mason-Dixon Line, I spent a significant portion of tenth grade learning about the Civil War. In addition to the moral issue of slavery, my teacher, Mr. Fahey, led us through York's history as a borderland where men fought for both the North and the South and indicted *both* sides for the economic, political, and social issues that separated the nation. When I moved to North Carolina for college, it took me a while to recognize that the War of Northern Aggression named the same events. This name reveals the still-raw and lingering (even after 147 years!)

memories of Union soldiers pillaging southern cities and of northern "carpetbaggers" exploiting the intended reconstruction. Perspectives changed again when I moved to northern Indiana and heard the events called the War Between the States. Indiana residents position themselves squarely in the "Heartland of America" and feel little if any attachment to the fringes, particularly the East Coast. Finally, a memorial in Harvard Square in Cambridge, Massachusetts, remembers the dead from the War to Preserve the Union. The personal and communal impact of the events that occurred between 1861 and 1865 is obvious in the ways four regions of the country name their experience of it.

Study, training, reflection, and experience are important aspects of preparing pastoral leaders for ministry. Still, no matter how well these have been done, failure will result if they have not also developed a contextual approach for determining whether and how to use their knowledge, skills, and tools in their settings. They need the ability to survey the elements that shape a faith community and influence members' interpretation of God's story. They also need an approach for integrating God's story with their own as well as to help others in their community to do the same. I call this approach "ecological understanding." It is a way to be attentive to the stories we keep as we add new chapters to our personal and communal stories. Sometimes the story we think we are in is different from the story we are actually in; a slight shift in perspective can significantly enhance our understanding. When teaching, I offer two additional stories to illuminate the formational effects of our environments as well as to caution leaders as they seek to create frameworks for keeping, sharing, and making new stories of faith.

Imagine a series of images that depict a package of watermelon seeds, cube-shaped watermelons, and a cube-shaped Plexiglas form.[1] The environment is also a type of container that creates formational opportunities and constraints. The package of watermelon seeds highlights one's potential, particularly when the environment is conducive

---

1. "Square Fruit Stuns Japanese Shoppers," June 15, 2001. *http://news.bbc.co.vk/2/hi/1390088.stm* (accessed August 13, 2012).

with good soil, proper fertilization, the right light, and a host of other elements. When I ask those viewing the seed image to imagine what results when the seeds are planted, participants typically provide rich descriptions of oblong-shaped melons with light and dark green stripes and the succulent red fruit with black seeds that appear when the melon is split. They also remember tales from their youth of family picnics, success during watermelon seed spitting and greased watermelon competitions, and delight as they describe juice running from mouth to chin. When I show the next image of a cube-shaped watermelon, there are typically audible gasps, and a few chuckles. Cube-shaped watermelons were unexpected. These unnatural forms were the result of commercial efforts to create a more manageable product to ship. As we discuss how the flowering bulb matured in a cube-shaped Plexiglas container, we also reflect on the ethical and moral implications of controlling environments, no matter what the intent.

The final story illustrates the way our environment conditions perception and often creates blinders that limit our ability to see. In 2010, Dubai proudly claimed the distinction of having the world's tallest manmade structure. Soaring over 2,700 feet into the air and costing over $1.5 billion, Burj Khalifa (Arabic for "Khalifa Tower") is a marvel of human achievement. It also reflects a fairly recent change in perspective. From the dawn of time until the late nineteenth century, the tallest buildings were only five or six stories tall, less than eighty feet. Although there were many methods to hoist containers to great heights with pulleys and ropes, most builders designed structures for life and work based on the number of floors a man (yes, a man) could carry supplies. Short-distance elevators existed since 1743 when King Louis XV had the first one-story passenger elevator, but there were no mechanisms to stop a free-falling platform, so they were rarely used to transport people. This changed in 1852 when Elisha Graves Otis invented the first safety elevator with hydraulic stoppers, but skyscrapers did not emerge until the 1880s. Some of the delay was because engineers needed to determine how to create structural steel that could hold greater loads and ways to provide heat, plumbing, and telephones in taller buildings. Over time, these innovations were available. The greater impediment to building skyscrapers was the human imagination. Architects in the 1850s and 1860s saw elevators as an easier way to move supplies up five or six stories; it took their children, who grew up *using* elevators, to envision skyscrapers.

As these stories highlight, contexts matter. They shape how we view the world and both open and close us to alternatives. We can reinterpret them and guide evangelization and formation efforts to more effectively create and maintain vital communities oriented toward God's mission by using an ecological approach. This framework highlights five digital age features that are causing disequilibrium and suggests ways faith communities can provide counterbalance.

ECOLOGICAL UNDERSTANDING

Commonly associated with "green" or environmental issues, *ökologie* or *oecology* was coined by German zoologist and philosopher Ernst Haeckel in 1866. Derived by combining the Greek *oikos*, meaning "home, household, or family," with the ending *-logy* from *logos*, meaning "discourse or systematic study," ecology literally means the study of the home or household. Haeckel used *ökologie* to emphasize the interrelation of all creation and to identify the specific characteristics each organism evolved in order to relate to other species and to thrive in its habitat.

Most well recognized within biology, ecology is the study of the interrelation between and among living and non-living habitat components. Viewed through a series of expanding relationships, these ecosystems include *organisms* (the smallest unit), *species* or *families* (a cluster of organisms), and *communities* (a cluster of families). Natural relationships develop between types of species in an ecology. *Native species* are original to an environment while *immigrant species* arrived from another environment. An *indicator species* is an organism whose presence, absence, or abundance reflects a specific environmental condition (i.e., canary in a mine) and a *keystone species* is an organism whose presence within an ecosystem has a disproportionate effect on other organisms within the system and whose role is critical to the maintenance and health of the system. These relationships also include different forms of interaction between species: *competition, predation* (predator-prey), *parasitic* (one organism benefits while harming another), *commensalism* (one organism benefits without impact on another), *mutualism* (both organisms benefit from relationship), *symbiosis* (relationships between different species), and *co-evolution* (reciprocal effect on each other's evolution).

Many disciplines are now using the language of an ecology to recognize the interdependence of elements within a complex system and to express shifts due to environmental influences.[2] In a mass-mediated context, communication was viewed primarily as transportation focusing on the delivery of content from a sender to a receiver and education was understood as a hierarchical transaction in which a "master" transmitted knowledge to students. In an interactive, networked context, communication is understood as a ritual that recognizes production and power dynamics and considers the formational character of the *entire* process. Similarly, education in an interactive age is a multimodal, collaborative process in which disciplines are integrative and meaning is communal.

Many analogies can be drawn using this schema. The next chapter focuses on the complex integration of elements operative when faith communities are keeping, sharing, and making stories as an ecology of faith. What must be underscored is their interdependence. An ecological perspective reminds us that the health

2. In mapping disciplinary thought, it is interesting that G.H. Mead and John Dewey, who emphasized educational ecology, taught Robert Park, who first used the term "human ecology" in 1921 to describe a branch of sociology that studies the relationships between a human community and its environment. Park taught Harold Innis who investigated the ecological impact of technology upon civilization. Innis and Marshall McLuhan were fellow faculty members at the University of Toronto. McLuhan taught Neil Postman who coined the term "media ecology" and initiated it as a field of study at NYU.

of *each* component affects the state of each organism and determines the health of the ecosystem. Thus, when one element within the system enters a state of *growth, stability,* or *decline,* there are ramifications—constructive and destructive—among the others. Ultimately, ecosystems seek equilibrium.

SEEKING EQUILIBRIUM

Equilibrium is defined as a state of balance in which the needs of each organism, the health and maintenance of each species, and the preservation or expansion of the ecosystem correlate. From its inception, Christianity has been an equilibrium-seeking force as its counter-cultural vision challenged prevailing assumptions and directions. Though he did not name it as such, theologian H. Richard Niebuhr catalogued five potential equilibrium-seeking responses of Christians to their culture in his 1951 classic, *Christ and Culture:*

- *Christ against Culture* shows Christianity and culture acting in opposition. Christians feel compelled to abandon the customs, institutions, and norms of society; call for a return to religious fundamentals; and encourage members to withdraw, either physically or practically, from a sinful world.
- *Christ of Culture* encourages assimilation and accommodation between Christianity and the world. In this model, Jesus works in concert with democratic principles to create a peaceful, cooperative society.
- *Christ above Culture* envisions Christ as a supernatural guide for human aspirations. Here Christ enters into the world to illuminate human potential, and Christianity is a path to elevate culture to its highest ideal.
- *Christ and Culture in Paradox* presents a dualistic tension. It recognizes the necessity and authority of both Christ and culture, but also their opposition. One believes that life can be lived in

tension between demands of Christ and culture in hope of justi-
fication, which lies beyond history.

- *Christ the Transformer of Culture* identifies culture as sinful, yet
believes it can be turned to Christian purposes. Focused on
conversion, proponents of this view start with the fallenness of
human beings and believe that transformation of the world is
possible through God's grace.

Careful to discount any implied judgment, Niebuhr's catalogue
was based on his experience of specific Christians of his day. He
identified the historical contexts that influenced Christians as they
responded to their world and challenged future believers to continue to do the same.

Today, individuals and organizations still seek equilibrium.
Within communities of faith there is a range of equilibrium deter-
minants, from those who seek universal belief, uniform practice,
and common agreement from all members, to those who focus on
mission and recognize the power of paradox and juxtaposition. In
my use within an ecology of faith, authentic dialogue and sustained
critical interaction measure equilibrium. In this conception, every
voice is valued, divergent views are respectfully received and seriously considered, and difference is often the site of personal conversion and social transformation.

When equilibrium is viewed as the balance of diverse perspectives
interacting, there are at least five digital age sites of imbalance that
could be corrected with the values and practices emphasized by vital
faith communities: paradigmatic blindness, generational distinctiveness
offset, communication methods, continuous partial attention, and
focus on physical places.

Blindness and Openness

Every message, religious or otherwise, is continually interpreted and
reinterpreted within a particular set of conditions. These culturally

specific criteria and classifications create a paradigm that is used as a frame of reference when we reflect on our experiences and construct meaning. Ecological factors influence interpretation and the meaning-making projected into an experience. These factors also affect what is seen and unseen.

Thomas Kuhn popularized the term "paradigm" in his classic treatise *The Structure of Scientific Revolutions*. By studying the way scientists are trained, Kuhn highlights two definitions of paradigm. In the first, paradigm is a shared mindset or worldview; it is a map that orients the community. In the second definition, paradigm is a model for how to operate within that mindset. It defines acceptable knowledge, beliefs, and practices. These are the map-maker's tools and reflect the process by which all are formed as we learn to maintain the map. The map shows paths to follow (or avoid) and the map-making tools predetermine ways to highlight (and hide) features. Both teach us what to see. As we accept what we learn from our elders and build upon their wisdom, we define the boundaries of what we can learn and call wisdom. Our paradigm shapes the questions we ask and the way we interpret the results we find. When our insights solve puzzles or further concepts *within* the paradigm—reinforcing current beliefs and practices—the community typically celebrates with applause and embrace; however, when we identify anomalies or suggest anything that is counter-cultural, insights are generally repressed and discounted, at least initially. Kuhn's *Copernican Revolution* illustrates this process with 1543 debates about the earth as the center of the universe and the forces that operated to maintain it as truth because of the catastrophic theological implications if it was not.[3]

Kuhn identifies four movements from the initial discounting of an anomaly to the subsequent embrace of a new paradigm. First, we

---

3. Thomas Kuhn, *The Structure of Scientific Revolutions* (Chicago: University of Chicago Press, 1962, 1970) and *Copernican Revolution* (Cambridge, MA: Harvard University Press, 1957).

begin in a given *paradigm* and maintain focus within its parameters until some disequilibrium broadens our worldview. Accumulating anomalies, unanswerable questions, and paradigm-challenging counter-instances initiate a time of *crisis,* an essential tension or unstable state that Kuhn identifies as the second movement. This crisis prepares us to interrogate previously blind adherence to a particular belief or practice. When unsuccessful tests and discounted hypotheses lead to the recognition that solutions are not within the confines of the original paradigm, we expand boundaries and begin to "see" differently, often revisiting discarded options instead of devising stories to eliminate any apparent conflict. This change of perspective is the third movement, *new sight.* The fourth movement is the inauguration of a *paradigm shift* that moves beyond the original paradigm's accepted norms to embrace an alternative. Kuhn's paradigmatic cycle concludes when the majority of the receiving community reconciles a *new paradigm* with the original and accepts the alternative.

TABLE 3: Paradigm Cycle

Stage	Definition	Function	Contribution
1. Paradigm	Map—mindset and model Methodology—mapmakers' tools	Orientation and framework to evaluate what is accepted and rejected Boundary	Provides common language and symbols Establishes common commitments Inspires common values and beliefs Maintains common exemplars
2. Crisis	Turning point Period of accumulating anomalies	Catalyst to recognize limits of paradigm Necessary (essential) tension	Generates openness to new approaches Inspires research outside paradigm

Continued

Continued

Stage	Definition	Function	Contribution
3. **New Sight**	Perspective change	Flash of intuition or insight that reorients *everything* Ability to "see" solution	Proposes new paradigm within which anomalies can be answered
4. **Paradigm Shift**	Period of revolutionary change	Time of initial resistance Appeals to continuity with past counter-balanced with articulation of supporting evidence for movement to a new paradigm	Replaces original paradigm with new paradigm via a revolution by degrees: first by an individual, then by a coalition within the community, followed by the whole community, culminating with the general populous
5. **New**	Map—mindset and model Methodology— mapmakers' tools	Orientation and framework to evaluate what is accepted and rejected Boundary	Provides common language and symbol Establishes common commitments Inspires common values and beliefs Maintains common exemplars

What is helpful in this cycle for pastoral leaders is the articulation of paradigmatic blindness. This concept of an individual or community's inability (and often unwillingness) to see another perspective or consider changing one's worldview highlights one of the greatest obstacles in creating and maintaining a vital community and a robust cycle of discipleship. Divergent views are raised as points of debate and competition, not dialogue and collaboration. For the health of the whole ecology, faith communities need to foster a spirit of relational openness.

A spirit of relational openness can breathe new life into a community by encouraging individuals to "learn to see" when they experience a disorienting dilemma or cognitive dissonance. It challenges them to reconsider assumptions and conclusions in light of the other's divergent view, and the understanding it engenders supports a choice to maintain one's perspective or shift in favor of an alternative view. This requires faith communities to develop a stance of relational openness toward anyone who identifies an anomaly as well as to establish an intentional process that appropriately surfaces divergent perspectives and encourages expansive thinking.

Generational Particularities

Age is one of the most significant paradigm-creating factors within a faith community. Unlike previous eras of human communication in which most generations were formed by the same dominant media, the twenty-first century is unique because it includes cohorts that were significantly shaped by each of the four eras of human communications. When not acknowledged by a faith community, *generational particularities* can become the second site of ecological imbalance. Activities that encourage *intergenerational discipleship* are a corrective that recognize the gifts and wisdom of each age and era as they inspire diverse expression and support right relations.

Sociologist Karl Mannheim first introduced the significance of birth cohort in his 1952 essay "The Problem of Generations."[4] Arguing that people exposed to similar geographic settings, time periods, and cultural phenomena have a shared vision of the world, he identified behavioral and attitudinal differences among adolescents born

---

4. Karl Mannheim, "The Problem of Generations" in *Essays on the Sociology of Knowledge* (New York: Oxford University Press, 1952).

during different time periods. Historians William Strauss and Neil Howe have continued Mannheim's efforts in their books.[5]

Noting common generational beliefs and behavior patterns that reflect a shared location in history, Howe and Strauss identify a remarkable repeating pattern over the past five centuries. They categorize these patterns into four recurring "turnings," cycles that reveal "specific social roles that condition how we perceive the world and act on those perceptions."[6] Reflecting definitive events and circumstances experienced during one's life, Howe and Strauss argue that individuals and corporate groups assume a generational persona. Formed in a matrix of cultural, social, political, religious, and economic conditions within the United States, Howe and Strauss christened recent generations as GI, Silent, Boomers, Gen X, and Millennials. From the perspective of evangelization and faith formation, three of these warrant particular attention.

Born between 1943 and 1960, Baby Boomers gained their name from the "fertility boom." The Vietnam War, the Civil Rights Movement, the sexual revolution, the space program, the birth control pill, Stonewall, and the Second Vatican Council—particularly for Roman Catholics—influenced them. Howe and Strauss highlight a shift from Boomers' youthful idealism to characterize their now judgmental and moralistic values including intolerance, narcissism, and hypocrisy.[7] On the whole, Boomers developed strong, stable families and experienced a wider gender-role gap than young people today. More

---

5. William Strauss and Neil Howe have continued Mannheim's efforts in their books: *13th Generation* (New York: Vintage Books, 1993); *The Fourth Turning* (New York: Broadway Books, 1997); and *Millennials Rising* (New York: Vintage Books, 2000). M. Rex Miller adds the effect of media in *The Millennium Matrix* (San Francisco: Jossey Bass, 2004).

6. Howe and Strauss, *The Fourth Turning*, 3, 16.

7. Howe and Strauss argue that historical events shape generational attitudes and behaviors and that generations shape history in *Millennials Rising*. Most of their generational descriptors parlay negative connotations, as illustrated here. See Howe, *Millennials*, 31–58, particularly 51–58. *The Fourth Turning* provides more nuanced identification describing the attitudinal and behavioral shifts that occur within a generation over a lifetime. For example, young adult Boomers are identified by values they defended—monogamy, thrift, continence—which by midlife are expressed with "fire-and-brimstone judgmentalism." Howe, *Turnings*, 224.

influenced by mass media print and radio, this group includes many current leaders including clergy, religious educators, and scholars.

The Americans with Disabilities Act and MTV influenced Gen Xers, born between 1961 and 1981, in addition to the Vietnam War and the Civil Rights Movement. Characterized by Strauss and Howe as self-centered, pessimistic, alienated, and impatient, this population included what popular culture identifies as the first "latchkey kids." Spawned by unpleasant memories of childhood, they heralded a "fertility bust," yet according to Howe and Strauss are emerging as more protective of their children, as evidenced by their embrace of home-schooling, telecommuting, and choosing extra time over extra pay. Born into the mass media television era, they were the first generation to use personal computers and the Internet as digital immigrants. Many faith community leaders are also in this group along with the rising population of "nones."

Born between 1982 and 2000, the third group goes by various names including Millennials, Gen Y, and NetGen. Technology, single-parent families, and global relationships have influenced their world. Described by Howe and Strauss as special, sheltered, confident, team-oriented, achieving, pressured, conventional, and optimistic, these young people are more numerous, more affluent, better educated, and more racially and ethnically diverse than any other generation. Touting reputations as social activists and collaborators, Howe and Strauss claim Millennials generally accept authority, follow rules, and are experiencing a narrower gender-role gap. They identify relatively unstable family structures that are strengthening. They are the first generation to grow up surrounded by digital technology.

In addition to divergent characteristics, Boomers, Gen Xers, and Millennials share three desires. The first coalescing force is a search for a *common ground*. With the philosophical and cultural changes heralded by postmodernity, and the cross currents they spawn, many people are searching for an interpretive framework by which to explore diverse experiences and ideas, in order to make meaning, and from which to make decisions. Often articulated as a desire for a clear set of standards or criteria, a community of faith's ability or inability to negotiate conflicting interpretations indicates whether or not the common ground will unite or divide the community. The second desire these individuals and groups often cite is longing for a common *place*. Although advances in transportation and communication have enabled a mobile workforce, they have created more transient populations. No longer connected to a ground-giving center (a neighborhood store, bar, community center, school, or church, for example), many individuals seek a place in which to develop and to maintain a sense of *identity and belonging*. Finally, whether or not they name it God, these populations typically seek a means to satisfy their hearts' unfulfilled *desires*. Visible in the myriad of spiritual quests is their desire for a connection with some higher power.[8] In response, communities of faith may offer that common ground, communal space, and a means to connect with God. Faith communities typically encourage opportunities for intergenerational interaction and provide a faith-based lens for interpretation and decision-making. As a result, relationships with a parish or congregation can initiate a sense of identity, foster belonging, and provide a forum for a corporate relationship with God.

Transmission to Ritual

The third site of ecological imbalance occurs when human communication is viewed simply as a form of transmission—getting a message from point A to point B. In contrast, ritual communications recognizes the way communications is a culture that creates a whole environment. This ecological view recognizes the impact of communications on a message, thus offering a counterbalance to a transmission view's inequity. Communications scholar James W. Carey introduced *ritual communications* to highlight formative qualities of

---

8. Originally from Merton Strommen's 1974 classic, *Five Cries of Youth* (San Francisco: Harper-Row, 1974), these themes continually emerge in denominational studies, i.e., Carroll's *The New Faithful*.

communication processes.[9] This view of communications is predicated on the belief that there are ongoing relationships that occur not only between the sender(s) and receiver(s), but also between and among all elements of the exchange: message, context, purpose, symbols/signs, meanings, history. It also recognizes that there are production and power dynamics that undergird these relationships, nuance the message(s), and affect the receiver(s) and sender(s). Thus, in addition to particularities about individuals (age, experience, interest in topic, etc.) and their movement in the cycle of discipleship (seeker, nominal adherent, active participant, etc.), other elements influence evangelization and faith formation.

Recall that meaning-making in the Interactive Age occurs through one's participation in a communicative process. The combination of story-keeping, story-sharing, and story-making emphasizes grounding stories of God's presence and the community's responses across time as is evident in the implicit and explicit, formal and informal, personal and communal, passive and interactive communicative practices of a community of faith. Engagement in the life of a physically present, intentional, and interactive faith community immerses community members in a multi-faceted and multi-sensory ecological system that links past with future. This ecology includes not only oral interaction, but also sights, sounds, smells, and textures that embody faith.

Every element of community life can be transformed from a transmission model of human communications to a ritual one. Self-defined as well as community-imposed leaders who function hierarchically as "the sage on the stage" and control communication are moving to a more collaborative view as "the guide on the side" who walks with and mentors other followers. Concurrently, community members can shift from passive recipients waiting in line at spiritual filling stations to active participants who understand that they are the Body of Christ and authors of new stories of faith. By thinking

---

9. James Carey, *Communication as Culture: Essays on Media and Society* (New York: Routledge, 1988), 18–19.

expansively about life in the faith community and ways to ritually share God's story, we can integrate all the actions of a community as opportunities for evangelization and faith formation.

Continuous Partial Attention to Sustained Critical Interaction

The fourth imbalance resulting from the interactive age is *continuous partial attention* (CPA). Technology innovator and educator Linda Stone coined the phrase in 1998 to describe "the increasing inability and undesire to pay full attention to just one task, item, or person and instead continually scan for other opportunities . . . while waiting for the next interruption." It describes how many individuals gain constant, instantaneous access to resources and relationships in a digital, networked environment. Stone differentiates CPA from multitasking by considering motivations. Multitasking is the performance of a variety of tasks at the same time with equal prioritization to increase productivity and efficiency; continuous partial attention is a constant, adrenaline-driven scan for and evaluation of ways to stay connected, regardless of how superficially. Related to FOMO (fear of missing out), Stone says CPA means "to be busy, to be connected, is to be alive, to be recognized, and to matter."[10]

Stone was the first to identify this interactive age characteristic and study its impact on humans' ability to concentrate and contemplate. In a current Apple commercial, mobile technology users simultaneously send and receive texts and tweets, research topics on the Internet, learn about breaking news, see who is in the vicinity, write a document, send an e-mail, check traffic congestion—all while meeting with an individual or group in one's home or office. Weighing contributions and limitations, Stone argues that continuous partial attention, in small doses, can be a very functional behavior; however, in large doses, it creates a stress-filled, over-stimulated life that

---

10. Linda Stone's website: *http://lindastone.net/qa/continuous-partial-attention* (accessed September 16, 2012).

can result in a sense of powerlessness and being unfulfilled as well as feeling isolated, even when connected.

More recently, Nicholas Carr asked "Is Google Making Us Stoopid?"[11] and popularized the notion that digital media and social networking are causing a loss in our ability to concentrate and sustain engaged thought. Using neuroscientific evidence, he argues in *The Shallows*[12] that the ways that we "think, read, and remember" are being changed by Internet use. More than Stone's assessment that individuals are *choosing* to partially engage in daily life, Carr is convinced that digital technologies are making it impossible for individuals to focus and fully engage.

Continuous partial attention and shallow thinking reveal two ecological imbalances. Some pastoral leaders fear that this is causing an inability to engage theological concepts and connect with God. Fortunately, communities of faith can offer rebalancing correctives. Sometimes we need to unplug, like Jesus going to the desert, to regain perspective. Whether short "minute meditations" or longer "retreats" from digital activity, there are countless alternatives for refreshment and renewal when digital culture becomes life-draining rather than life-enhancing.

Sustained critical interaction is another option faith communities can use to moderate the potential effects of wired life on deep thinking. Rather than fear a loss of engagement with abstract theological concepts, pastoral leaders can encourage activities that ensure continued dialogue, theological reflection, and integration over time. It requires a commitment to remain in relationship. For example, sustained interaction with seekers and nominal members may be more intense. They are more like young people who want to get to know each other better as they decide if a permanent commitment is desirable. For active participants, sustained interaction is likely more regular and predictable: weekly worship, midweek workshop, monthly meeting. For those who want to delve into theological education, sustained interaction may

---

11. Nicholas Carr, "Is Google Making Us Stoopid?" (*The Atlantic,* August 2008).
12. Nicholas Carr, *The Shallows* (New York: W. W. Norton, 2010).

take a variety of forms, mixing personal and communal engagement in onsite and online forums. For someone experiencing a time of crisis, there is likely extensive contact in a brief burst, and when someone is absent—either physically missing or whose voice has been silenced—someone in the community initiates reintegration. Regardless of role or context, sustained interaction in a community of faith provides care and nourishment for people, meeting them where they are and inviting them into deeper relationships with one another and with God.

It is unfortunate that the word "critical" has gained personally directed connotations of severe (and often excessive) judgment instead of its use as focused attention and careful analysis. Requiring a shift from partial attention, it recognizes that knowledge carries with it responsibility and invites conversation partners to consider the social, political, and economic forces operative within and across divergent views. The hope is to evoke change and orient participants toward life-supporting praxis. A necessary element of personal conversion and social transformation, critical interaction is generally a catalyst that sparks the circle of conversion and ignites members along the cycle of discipleship.

In a faith context, interaction defines how community members are self-reflective stewards of their own gifts and needs as well as identifies the essential character of one's active engagement with others and the community's texts, traditions, rituals, symbols, and artifacts. It is a mutual, reciprocal way of knowing that can also be called dialogue. Reflecting Martin Buber's insight, "genuine dialogue" is a search for *understanding,* not necessarily agreement, which can occur when interaction is grounded by relational openness.

> Genuine dialogue—no matter whether spoken or silent—is where each of the participants really has in mind the other or others in their present and particular being and *turns* to them with the intention of establishing a living mutual relation between himself (or herself) and them.[13]

---

13. Martin Buber, *Between Man and Man* (New York: The MacMillan Co, 1947), 19.

More than simply assuring that the community's stories, signs, meanings, values, and priorities are shared from peer to peer and from one generation to the next, this form of interaction becomes the catalyst for and site of personal conversion and social transformation. Buber claims that by turning, these participants meet on a "narrow ridge" that establishes presence of one with another. The dynamic that occurs in the in-between is what is central to evangelization and faith formation. In that liminal space of "between," where an "I" engages a "You," both transform and are transformed.

Physical Place to Digital Space

Finally, a shift from *physical place* to *digital space* poses a challenge. As I am encouraging Christians to unplug and to retreat from constant digital connectivity, I want to support creating and sustaining a virtual presence. Maintaining equilibrium as the convergence of voice, video, and data impact every aspect of human life means that there is a growing need to blend activities in physical places with efforts in digital spaces. This is the new frontier for evangelization and faith formation.

In the twenty-first century, if you do not have a web presence, you do not exist. Faith communities need to be online to be considered, and to be considered relevant. From an evangelization perspective, faith communities that claim a virtual space can ensure that God's Word is heard and God's mission is visible for all creation. Once the interest of seekers is gained and new members welcomed, faith communities need to share the stories and traditions they have kept and encourage others to make them anew. It is not always possible for people to gather physically together due to competing demands and interests. In response, many church leaders are looking outward, beyond the church walls, to identify ways to meet the needs of God's people and support them in their faith practices. Thinking outside the box, some are embracing interactive digital technologies to create *virtual spaces* for everything from Bible study and theological discussions to virtual worship.

When considering the development of a virtual presence, it is vital that communities carefully identify the elements of personal and communal life that *must* occur in physically gathered places and those that could be moved to digital spaces. One of the most widespread critiques of digital interaction is the disembodied nature of online relationships. Fearing contact with others who may misrepresent themselves and defending the need for physical, particularly sensory, engagement, many argue that communities cannot exist virtually and online worship is not "real." Sacramental communities, particularly those that feature receiving bread and wine at the Eucharist as the hallmark of worship, cannot conceive of a way to experience God's presence in the sacrament online.

Concerns like these prompted religious communications professor Stephen O'Leary to share his views in "Cyberspace as Sacred Space." First published in 1996, it is widely heralded as the earliest essay to explore the implications of Internet-mediated communications for religious institutions, predicting a liturgical evolution parallel to the one which resulted from the simultaneous introduction of the printing press and the Protestant Reformations. Tapping insights gained from his 1994 study of CompuServe forums (pre-Internet virtual spaces for chat-like interaction) that met at preordained times for prayer and Scripture study, he found that most participants engaged in collective practices much as they would in a real church and that their interaction provided a more intimate connection than he realized was possible. Referencing philosopher of language John Searle's "sincerity condition," he argues that the degree to which one *believes* affects the efficacy of the rituals.[14] Thus, applying O'Leary's insights to an analysis of virtual practices, the question may not be "Can God be present in virtual sacraments?" as much as "Do the real-life people interacting in virtual spaces *believe* God is there?"

14. Stephen O'Leary, "Cyberspace as Sacred Space," first published in *Journal of the American Academy of Religion* (Vol. 64, No. 4, Winter 1996); Lorne L. Dawson, Douglas E. Cowan, *Religion Online: Finding Faith on the Internet* (New York: Routledge, 2004) 53–54.

Regardless of individual and communal positions about digitally mediated interaction, the wholesale elimination of these technologies discards a significant resource that, with care, can extend faith community evangelization and formation efforts. As we consider *appropriate* advances into this new virtual world, success will be measured by whether or not seekers and faith community members can hear God's word, grow in faith, and experience God's presence.

BALANCE BELIEF AND PRACTICE

An ecology of faith recognizes strength in a community of faith that provides an orienting vision (story-keeping), maintains a prophetic voice through sustained critical interaction (story-sharing), and responds by seeking opportunities for personal conversion and social transformation (story-making). Grounding these equilibrium-seeking practices is a key principle: what a faith community says it believes should match how it operates—and vice versa. Vitality in a faith community includes a balance between hearing the Word and living the Word, between thought and action. The espoused equals the operative.

There is no easy way to reach our fullest potential as individuals or as a community. It takes time and dedication to know the story of God's action in our lives and to believe God's life-transforming love is readily available. It takes even more time and dedication to develop relationships with God, self, others, and all creation that embody and enact that understanding. To begin, faith communities need to create safe, hospitable spaces that encourage appropriate vulnerability and genuine respectful dialogue. One of the greatest obstacles to this type of interaction is fear, particularly of that which is unknown or other. Developing an environment and process to help individuals "talk across difference" can foster understanding and initiate the Dream of God.

There are many techniques for cultivating life-giving and life-sustaining relationships where what one says he or she believes is practiced. One of the most effective processes I have experienced was developed by Valerie Batts and offered by VISIONS, Inc., the company she co-founded to consult and train in diversity and inclusion (*http://www.visions-inc.org/vis-consultants.htm*). They have designed immersive experiences to unpack assumptions and prejudices that include two elements I want to highlight. The first begins the process of teaching inclusion by demonstrating ways to welcome and support every participant using VISIONS's core set of guidelines and adding to them. These seemingly simple adages prove more complex in practice and include: "try on new ideas, content, and processes"; "it's ok to disagree—it's not ok to shame, blame, or attack yourself or others"; "practice self-focus"; "practice both/and thinking"; "take responsibility for your own learning"; "maintain confidentiality"; and "beware of the difference between intent and impact." The second was designed to help us see different levels of engagement and ensure that our reactions and responses were to the appropriate source. They include:

- personal—attitudes, beliefs, opinions
- interpersonal—behaviors, treatments, and relationships
- institutional—policies, practices, and systems
- cultural—values, norms, and expression

To attain balance between what communities say they believe and how they practice, communities of faith will benefit by using some form of guidelines to recognize and talk across difference.

⊗ further reflection

- Contexts matter. They shape us and our stories. They influence our ability to recognize and interpret our stories. Have you had the experience of "not seeing" or "seeing differently" than others as you have kept, shared, and made new stories? What has helped you learn to see?
- Ecology is the study of the relationship between and among living and non-living habitat components. An ecological perspective

illuminates the variety of species and types of relationships that can occur in an environment. How would you describe your community using these concepts that describe different types of species: *native, immigrant, indicator,* and *keystone*, and the forms of interaction between them: *competition, predation* (predator-prey), *parasitic* (one organism benefits while harming another), *commensalism* (one organism benefits without impact on another), *mutualism* (both organisms benefit from relationship), *symbiosis* (relationships between different species), and *co-evolution* (reciprocal effect on each other's evolution)?

- Ecologies are generally in a state of *growth, stability,* or *decline* and ecological systems seek equilibrium. How would you describe the state of your faith community and evaluate your efforts to maintain balance?

- This chapter identifies five ways faith communities can offer equilibrium-seeking counter balances to features of the interactive age. Are any of these operative in your community of faith? Are there any that you would add?

- One of the most challenging questions pastoral leaders face as they consider moving online is stated explicitly as *"Is virtual church real?"* This implies the question, *"Is God present?"* My goal has been to challenge us to recognize God in our midst, even online, and to prayerfully discern individual and collective responses to this brave, new, albeit virtual world. Do you think God can be present online?

- What elements are necessary in your context to "talk across difference"?

 Continue the conversation online at
http://faithformation4-0.com.

→ 6

Faith Formation as an Ecology of Faith

For just as the body is one and has many members, and all the members of the body, though many, are one body, so it is with Christ. For in the one Spirit we were all baptized into one body—Jews or Greeks, slaves or free—and we were all made to drink of one Spirit. Indeed, the body does not consist of one member but of many. If the foot were to say, "Because I am not a hand, I do not belong to the body," that would not make it any less a part of the body. And if the ear were to say, "Because I am not an eye, I do not belong to the body," that would not make it any less a part of the body. If the whole body were an eye, where would the hearing be? If the whole body were hearing, where would the sense of smell be? But as it is, God arranged the members in the body, each one of them, as he chose. If all were a single member, where would the body be? As it is, there are many members, yet one body. The eye cannot say to the hand, "I have no need of you," nor again the head to the feet, "I have no need of you." On the contrary, the members of the body that seem to be weaker are indispensable, and those members of the body that we think less honorable we clothe with greater honor, and our less respectable members are treated with greater respect;

Continued

whereas our more respectable members do not need this. But God has so arranged the body, giving the greater honor to the inferior member, that there may be no dissension within the body, but the members may have the same care for one another. If one member suffers, all suffer together with it; if one member is honored, all rejoice together with it. 1 Corinthians 12:12–26

Most faith-claiming people, particularly those under fifty, do not explicate doctrinal formulas or creedal statements when asked to describe their experience of faith formation or religious education. Instead, they typically tell stories. Often they share insights from wisdom keepers in their families or memorable experiences with friends on retreats, mission trips, or other communal gatherings. Beyond humorous anecdotes, many reveal theological understanding gained by participation in the life of the faith community. Some are narratives of faith-filled activities: embodying the Christian story by participating in a Christmas pageant or Passion play, engaging Scripture and other expressions of faith through song with the choir, responding to communal needs by making cookies for the weekly supper for the homeless, or rebuilding homes. Some stories chronicle insights gleaned from others informally during coffee hour and formally in regularly occurring classes and workshops.

Accounts of faith-forming experiences often relate to seasons: marking time in anticipation of Christmas by lighting the pink and purple candles of an evergreen-laden Advent wreath; welcoming the Baby Jesus with song while gathered around a crèche with figures of the holy family, the shepherds, and the magi at Christmas; holding iron railroad nails on Good Friday and reflecting on how they may resemble those hammered through Jesus' hands and feet; and ringing bells, smelling incense, and singing the Gloria for the first time in forty days to acknowledge the Resurrection at Easter. Sometimes the tales relate to sacraments: learning about the eucharistic meal while serving on the altar, understanding initiation into a community after witnessing a full emersion baptism and a Lion-King-like presentation of a bare-skinned babe to the community, or remembering Jesus' last days while being fed and nourished through communion.

As these vignettes illustrate, stories are a way that faith communities keep the essential elements of who they are (identity) and whose they are (belonging). When shared, they highlight the essential function of being immersed in an environment that inspires meaning-making[1] and provide glimpses of the transformative qualities of participation with and within a faith community. These multisensory, multi-modal elements and activities highlight Maria Harris's belief from *Fashion Me A People:* "The church does not have an educational program, it is one."[2]

Harris's focus is what happens within a faith community. She shows how a constellation of prayer and worship, teaching and learning, guidance and healing, service and outreach, enablement and advocacy create an immersive environment that passes on the faith, almost by osmosis. She does so by recognizing the ancient combination of roles and functions which the earliest church disciples practiced from Acts 2:1–45: *koinonia* (community-building), *didache* (teaching), *leiturgia* (prayer/worship), *kerygma* (priestly listening, prophetic speech, and political advocacy), and *diakonia* (serving/ministering). This is an ecological system that identifies the characteristics that enable a faith community to guide practitioners to a deeper awareness of God's presence and action in their lives, and motivates

1. "Meaning making," as religious educator Jane Regan reminds in her book *Toward an Adult Church: A Vision of Faith Formation* (Chicago: Loyola Press, 2002), "refers to the fundamental activity of human being. To be human is to engage in the process of finding the patterns and forms and relationships that give unity and significance to one's life. It is the process of seeking coherency and meaningfulness in the elements of human existence. Every act of perception is an act of meaning making; it is a composing of reality" (32).

2. Maria Harris, *Fashion Me A People: Curriculum in the Church* (Louisville, KY: Westminster/John KnoxPress, 1989), 47.

them to live in such a way that, individually and collectively, all move closer to enacting the Dream of God.

Within the United States, this environmental system that functionally formed Christians was not limited to activities within a faith community. In *America Religion and Religions,* religious studies professor Catherine Albanese describes how the religious motivations of the United States' founders influenced America's development as a religious nation. She explores the way the American ethos creates a civil religion by first introducing "The Four Cs":

- *Creeds* explain the meaning or meanings of human life, which might be systematic theologies, oral traditions, narratives, and so forth.
- *Codes* or rules govern everyday behavior and range from complex systems of laws to unwritten customs and general ethical ideas.
- *Cultuses* or rituals act out the understandings and insights of the creeds and codes.
- *Communities* unite people to a shared identity through common creed(s), code(s) and cultus(es). These might be formal or informal. They could take the form of ethnic or cultural groups or formal institutions such as churches, denominations, etc.

Albanese uses the four Cs to develop a compelling working definition of religion as "a system of symbols (creed, code, cultus) by means of which people (a community) orient themselves in the world with reference to both ordinary and extraordinary powers, meanings, and values."[3] She then shows how the "manyness" of different religious traditions coexist in American society and creates a religious "oneness" expressed through a common culture rooted in Anglo-Protestantism. From this view, the impact of an "American civil religion" is evident.

During most of the last century within the United States, efforts to proclaim the gospel and make Christians was simultaneously communicated by rich religiously oriented beliefs and practices

---

3. Catherine Albanese, *America Religion and Religions* (Covington, KY: Wadsworth, 1981), 9.

embedded in both the life of the faith community and the American culture. Social norms and civic practices functioned—formally and informally—to support Christian values. Religious literacy—the general population's understanding of religious systems and the language they use to share beliefs and practices—was high in large measure because secular institutions and public conversations often referenced Christian stories.

In his book *Will Our Children Have Faith,*[4] Episcopal priest and religious educator John Westerhoff showed how a Protestant ethos was dominant in public schools, the media, the government, and civic circles, particularly in the 1950s to 1970s. At that time, prayer was present in public schools, religious programming was popular in mass media—print, radio, and television—and religious rituals and symbols were incorporated in public meetings and city events. As early as 1755, "blue laws" existed in New York and Connecticut to protect Sunday as a day of rest and worship. These laws reinforced religious standards by prohibiting things on Sundays like the sale of alcoholic beverages and restricting the hours that stores could be open. In effect, the *whole* environment functioned as part of an ecology of faith and supported Christian evangelization and formation efforts. In this context, faith communities could assume that the general population knew about Christianity and pastoral leaders could focus on the faith community, typically through worship and Sunday School or some other form of Christian education.

THE ECOLOGY IS BROKEN

In the twenty-first century this ecology is broken. Today, as post-colonial and post-modern sensitivities lead to increased integration of and respect for the diversity of religious and spiritual expressions as well as non-church perspectives, Christians cannot (and likely

---

4. John Westerhoff, *Will Our Children Have Faith* (Harrisburg, PA: Morehouse, 2012, 2000, 1976).

should not) assume reinforcement of their unique religious values in secular contexts. Cities and towns have eliminated public school prayer and religious displays after unconstitutional rulings by the U.S. Supreme Court. Religious radio and television programming has shifted from network-supported stories designed to uplift and nourish the human spirit to paid programming purchased primarily by evangelicals for worship services and talk shows. Even Sunday morning's focus on Christian worship has faded as blue laws have been repealed and a myriad of other opportunities compete for attention.

Although the Christianity-focused ecology of societal elements that Albanese and Westerhoff described no longer exists, most churches still operate as if it does and have not changed their practices. The majority of church services continue to be offered on Sunday morning and well-intentioned church members wait to provide hospitality to new people they hope will enter their church structures. Increasingly, faith communities are the lone source communicating faith themes, and the gap between those who are active church members and the rest of society is widening. Significant portions of the general population no longer know or understand Christian stories, traditions, and practices and many of those who are committed to a faith community are finding it impossible to be active in their church. Adults and youth alike experience the tension of conflicting expectations and values as the workweek extends late into the evening and weekend and school sports are often scheduled on Sunday mornings. Challenged to find one hour to attend Sunday worship, it is unlikely that they will participate in church activities interspersed through the week. In this new normal, opportunities to hear the gospel and learn of Jesus' way are forfeited and the time to integrate personal stories with faith stories is lost. For those who value the collections of Christian wisdom, identity-defining creeds, character-creating behavior codes, and time-crossing ritual practices, this is a time to reexamine assumptions and adjust practices. Our challenge is to spend time understanding the web of relationships that operate to form people in faith and reflect together on ways to appropriately utilize available resources to cultivate faith in the digital age.

As described in chapter five, ecology is the study of the interrelation between and among living and non-living habitat components in an environment. These ecosystems include organisms, species or families, and communities that develop different types of relationships: native, immigrant, indicator, and keystone. These species interact through competition, predation, parasitism, commensalism, mutualism, symbiosis, and co-evolution. The essential element to underscore is the interdependence of elements. The health of *each* component affects the state of each organism and determines the health of the ecosystem. Thus, when one element within the system enters a state of growth, stability, or decline, there are ramifications— constructive and destructive—among the others.

Many disciplines have begun to use ecological frameworks and analogies to explore complex integrations of elements. Bonnie Nardi and Vicki O'Day's *Information Ecologies* utilize ecological referents to analyze human-media interactions and their subsequent formative influences. They define information ecology as "a system of people, practices, values and technologies in a particular local environment" that is sustained by "the active, intelligent participation of the people involved in them."[5] They use the term "ecology" analogically to recognize that information ecologies, like biological ones, are complex systems that exhibit five primary characteristics. First, information ecologies are *systemic* and maintain strong interrelationship and dependencies among parts and elements. Second, they are *diverse* with many different kinds of niches, roles, and functions that spur natural opportunities for growth and success permitting the ecology to survive and adapt. Third, ecological components *co-evolve*, migrating and changing to fill available niches, roles, and functions, due to constraints and opportunities. Fourth, information ecologies create a

---

5. Bonnie Nardi and Vicki O'Day, *Information Ecologies* (Cambridge, MA: MIT Press, 1999), 50–51.

locality, established by members' participation and commitment to a set of shared motivations and values, that instills a sense of identity. Finally, the *keystone species,* identified as a "presence crucial to the survival of the ecology itself," maintains the ecosystem.

Nardi and O'Day use these properties in ethnographic studies of offices, libraries, schools, and hospitals to analyze the communicative tools applied in given situations, and to evaluate their effectiveness, appropriateness, and influence. This ecological perspective illuminates the sources of community development, the need for diversity and integration of unique elements within an ecosystem, the processes for individual and collective growth and adaptation, the development of a communal identity related to a sense of place or space, and the role of leaders. Expanding upon Nardi and O'Day's information ecology, evangelization and faith formation can also be viewed as ecology.

AN ECOLOGY OF FAITH

An ecology of faith includes systemic, individual, and communal features. Viewed as a religious system, an ecology of faith adds a fifth component—*collection*—to Catherine Albanese's "four Cs" that define a religion: *creed, code, cultus,* and *the community.* This addition recognizes the source of creeds, codes, and cultus in the community's collected stories. Grounded within this system, practitioners and members make commitments to God, to themselves, to the community, and to all creation as they live in faith. These include a covenant to be in sustained, lifelong engagement with one's faith, to participate fully as an active contributor within the community, and to live as a faith-filled witness within the world. Correlatively, the community provides an environment that encourages and enables member health and maturity. It offers an orienting paradigm, co-evolution-inspiring diversity, and an identity-generating locality. This ecology of faith inspires and supports companions on life's journey with a larger vision: the Dream of God.

A Religious System

Faith communities operate as a religious system with implicit and explicit components. Recognized within evangelization and faith formation efforts, faith communities develop context-sensitive, multimodal processes to express a self-defining collection of oral and written texts and traditions, creeds that draw from that collection to offer explanations about the meaning of human life in the universe, codes that govern behavior and establish a community's moral, ethical, and behavioral expectations, and cultus that orients a community to God through multi-sensory rituals, gestures, signs, and symbols. Together, these elements inculcate grounding stories, doctrinal tenets, and interpretative schemas that orient practitioners in the world as well as establish boundaries that both unite adherents and distinguish non-members. They also spur and guide individual and collective action.

This community-forming combination of collection, creed, code, and cultus involves the whole person, calling on all human faculties: body, mind, senses, imagination, emotion, and memory. Building on one of performance theory's[6] major insights, religion and ritual studies scholar Catherine Bell argues that this type of engagement in and with religious rituals and practices are more than "simply a means of transmitting ideas or molding attitudes, either by explicit socialization or implicit coding." Instead performance approaches show "how activities *create* culture, authority, transcendence, and whatever forms of holistic ordering are required for people to act in meaningful and

---

6. Catherine Bell traces the concept and use of performativity from its introduction as an interdisciplinary approach in the 1960s, through its establishment in critical discourse in the 1980s and 1990s, until today. She recounts that the use of religious language to describe non-sacred practices initiated much debate among academics in the later part of the twentieth century. Performance theory emerged due to concern about an implied universality of religion and a globalization of symbolic intentionality, particularly when the term "ritual" was used. This enables the use of ritual language in reference to sacred events and the use of performance theory to study a ritual's effect. See Catherine Bell, "Performance," in Mark C. Taylor, ed., *Critical Terms for Religious Studies* (Chicago & London: Chicago University Press, 1998), 205–224.

effective ways."[7] Through stories, traditions, prayers, worship, lament, healing, justice, and service, community members begin to embody and enact the faith community's vision.

Because community is an essential dimension, one cannot be or become a Christian in isolation. This premise requires commitments from both individuals who want to be or become Christian as well as from communities of faith that want to invite and form seekers and baptized members. Though presented as separate characteristics, these personal and communal commitments are interdependent. Communities of faith cannot maintain a vital ecosystem without the active participation of each individual and vice versa.

Personal Characteristics

As a relational system, an ecology of faith is most stable and thriving when those participating in the community make a set of commitments to God, to themselves, to a faith community, and to all of creation. These commitments are oriented toward establishing equilibrium—right relations. Typically tied to baptismal covenants within Christian communities, the goal is for members to establish a relationship with God through Jesus Christ that becomes the lens that orients their perspective and assists their decision-making. The hope is that one's relationships with God, oneself, others, and all creation motivate actions that further and foster the Dream of God.

Growing in faith always will be unique for each individual; there is no blueprint to direct one's process for developing a relationship with God or being a Christian. Still, theorists agree that personal growth and faith formation are most effective when participation is voluntary and self-directed, and has transformation-oriented goals.[8]

---

7. Bell, "Performance," 208.

8. Jane Regan's chapter on "The Adult as Person of Faith" is an excellent summary and critique of the behavioral, developmental, and constructivist models of formation. Regan, *Toward An Adult Church: A Vision of Faith Formation* (Chicago: Loyola Press, 2002), 30–70.

As seekers, initiates, and lifetime members mature through participation in the circle of conversion and cycle of discipleship, they support and maintain a thriving faith community. Colleagues, friends, and peers are benefited as one deepens a relationship with God through diverse opportunities that may include Bible studies and faith sharing groups, private prayer and corporate worship, spiritual direction and service-oriented outreach. These commitments require personal commitments of *time and attention.*

Sustained critical interaction is a means for participants to grow in faith with others. Aware that a faith community's operative paradigms provide orienting maps and map-making directions, this engagement enables individuals to navigate the chaos of contemporary society and to apply the community's wisdom in their life choices. Relational openness, a willingness to ask critical questions and a desire to vulnerably respond, enable mutual relationships to develop and mature. More than simply descriptive questions of analysis, observation, focus, and feeling, authentic faith-filled relationships share "dig deeper" questions that reveal God's mission and motivate a response. These questions explore vision, meaning, and change; consider consequences, obstacles, and alternatives; take personal inventory, contemplate theological principles, and recognize social responsibilities. Through genuine dialogue, conversation partners also can interject personal wisdom into communal life, thus assuring communal awareness of diverse perspectives and interpretations.

Communal Characteristics

Ideally, faith communities provide a reliable set of characteristics to seekers, adherents, and members. A particular *locality* provides a place or space for genuine dialogue and mutual interaction where those who communally gather are formed. Together they share a tradition or *orienting paradigm* (Christianity) through which they see and make meaning. To encourage personal conversion and social transformation, exemplary communities strive for *diversity*—in membership, thought, experience, expression, and response. When these characteristics operate as a healthy ecosystem, *co-evolution* results.

Within an ecological framework, *locality* recognizes contributions of both *place* (tangible, finite, physical) and *space* (intangible, infinite, virtual). Acknowledged as sites of identity-formation and shared values, faith communities maintain influence in at least three types of place or space. Generally grounded by a physical "home," the first is the community's gathering place.[9] A place of worship in most faith contexts, this location is typically the epicenter of all activity and touches the greatest proportion of the faith community. The second locality is personal and includes the unique cluster of social and religious institutions that an individual draws upon to grow in faith. It may include one's family, school, government, media, cultural center, and/or other spiritual, religious, and denominational resources. The third locality recalls that evangelization and faith formation occur in any *space* in which God's presence is recognized and message is heard—*everywhere* faith community members congregate and call on God's name.

These localities are most effective as sites of evangelization and formation when they provide at least five interrelated dimensions. As sites of hospitability, they should welcome a variety of members, contents, processes, and interpretations. As sites of sustained, intentional interactions, they encourage ongoing conversations and authentic, genuine dialogue between critically reflective, actively engaged individuals. As a holding environment, they provide safe spaces that

---

9. Historically, enculturating communities—both religious and not—meet in tangible, physical settings. In *The Great Good Place: Cafes, Coffee Shops, Bookstores, Bars, Hair Salons, and Other Hangouts at the Heart of a Community* (New York: Paragon House, 1991), Ray Oldenburg develops the concept that there are three essential places in people's lives. These are the places we live, work, and gather for conviviality. The third space is where communities can come into being and hold together. Many adults can identify a site—a local parish, a grandparent's home, the community store, a neighborhood bar, a youth center—that stood as the hub and catalyst for all activity. Through stories shared, these meeting grounds—touchstones for young and old to disembark and return telling their tales—provided meaning, direction, and inspiration and served as sites of initiation, orientation, commissioning, support, and proclamation.

perpetuate communal memory, foster dynamic interpreting and reinterpreting as well as creative imagining and re-imagining of the community's stories, and support participants as operative understandings of faith and life are challenged and transformed. Within a Christian context, the hope is that these localities encourage catalytic, other-oriented, grace-filled transformations.

Communities of faith generally orient adherents toward a particular interpretation of the community's collection, creed, code, and cultus. The operative paradigm can be static (fixed, unchangeable, immutable dogmatic teachings) or dynamic (a tradition open to interpretation and reinterpretation) and becomes the lens through which the community defines itself and its mission. In a healthy ecology, communities seek a balance between continuity and change using interpretive methods to assess current and future decisions and directions. As religious educator Mary Elizabeth Moore defines in *Educating for Continuity and Change: A New Model for Christian Religious Education*, continuity assures an unbroken chain of connectedness across time and space linking Jesus and his followers' founding communities with ours while change allows for transformation, conversion, and renewal.[10] She recommends a schema that includes Scripture, tradition, empirical data, and personal experience to ground members of a community of faith and balance continuity and change. This combination empowers individuals and corporate bodies to initiate meaningful engagement with and critique of their community's operative paradigm using story-keeping, story-sharing, and story-making practices. It also adds a valuable interpretive guide for faithful people trying to sort through the cacophony of information, resources, and choices in the twenty-first century.

The third and fourth communal characteristics in an ecological framework consist of *diversity* and *co-evolution*. Diversity, reflected here in that which is "other," generally challenges operative paradigms

---

10. Mary Elizabeth Moore, *Educating for Continuity and Change: A New Model for Christian Religious Education* (Nashville: Abingdon, 1983), 21–22.

and practices and can be a person, idea, belief, doctrine, practice, attitude, idea, symbol, artifact, context, and other catalyst. It also relates to those things emphasized when distinguishing one group of people from another including gender, race, ethnicity, class, religion, language, family lineage, nationality, cultural heritage, and age. By engaging difference, someone who is grounded by a particular paradigm becomes aware of an alternative and one's responsibility toward it. If they are open and willing to *fully* interact with the other—whether human or inanimate—considering difference with honesty and integrity and seeking understanding, the resulting tension opens individuals and communities to contemplate a change of *modus operandi*. This prompts evolutionary movement.

Integrally linked, diversity is required for the ecology's health and typically is the catalyst for co-evolution. Developmental psychologist Robert Kegan defines evolution as "a lifetime activity of differentiating and integrating what is taken as self and what is taken as other" and the corresponding change in meaning-making that results.[11] Similar in affect to Piaget's cognitive dissonance, a crisis typically initiates personal and communal transformation and starts a domino-like process whereby as one aspect of the ecology changes, others also turn, until the whole ecosystem is reoriented and renewed. Within faith communities, evolution reflects relational openness and willingness to engage the other. It assures ecological dynamism that dispels stagnation and inspires vitality.

Critical Intersections

The intersection of the systemic, individual, and communal components in an ecology of faith exposes two additional critical elements: sustained critical interaction and the keystone species. Sustained critical interaction asks a group of people to commit to an ongoing,

---

11. Robert Kegan, *The Evolving Self: Problem and Process in Human Development* (Cambridge, MA: Harvard University Press, 1982), 76–77.

intentional process of reflective engagement with a topic to determine whether and how to respond. As part of the ecosystem's complex process of communication, this is the catalyst for co-evolution through personal conversion and social transformation; it also enables the community to regain a state of equilibrium after such a life-altering change. The mechanism that ensures that sustained critical conversations occur and adjustments to maintain health and vitality over time are made in the ecosystem is the keystone species.

Sustained critical interaction describes how members are self-reflective agents that actively engage one another and the community's texts, traditions, rituals, symbols, and artifacts. It is a mutual, reciprocal way of knowing that can move participants from particular standpoints to gain insight in areas that they had not considered prior to engagement. More than simply assuring that the community's stories, signs, meanings, values, and priorities are shared from peer to peer and one generation to the next, this form of genuine dialogue becomes the catalyst for and site of personal conversion and social transformation.

The inclusion of the term "critical" intentionally incorporates *conscientization* into the process of engagement. Coined by Paulo Freire and embraced by liberation- and emancipation-oriented movements, conscientization represents the awakening of critical consciousness. Thus, a sustained critical interaction recognizes the social, political, and economic forces operative within and across countervailing views, focuses on social as well as political responsibility, and orients personal and collective interaction toward life-supporting praxis. Sustained critical interaction can ensure equilibrium; however, from an ecological perspective, a faith community needs a keystone species to help regulate the thermostat. Within communities of faith, this keystone species interprets the state of the ecosystem by not only helping members to know *what* to see, but also *how* to engage critically what is seen in order to avoid restrictive, destructive, and oppressive forces and decisions.

The keystone species is a presence crucial to the community's survival, and both orients and directs life in an ecosystem.

Ultimately, within a Christian community of faith, that guiding presence is God as revealed through Jesus Christ and the Holy Spirit. In baptism, all Christians become members of the Body of Christ who share responsibility for proclaiming the gospel and making Christians. We all share in the roles and functions of the keystone species as we participate in the circle of conversion and the cycle of discipleship. We are each invited to share leadership, which as Marshal Ganz, Kennedy School of Government at Harvard University Senior Lecturer, contends, "is accepting responsibility for enabling others to achieve purpose in the face of uncertainty." But we are not all members of the keystone species. Members of the keystone species emerge and act as catalytic guides who support the rest of the community as they embrace their faith and grow in it. These members may have formal designations like clergy and lay church professionals as well as informal roles like parents as the primary educators and community wisdom-keepers. Their role is to ensure that community members have the opportunity to experience God's presence as well as mature in faith and contribute to the community and in the world. As they develop relationships with people in the community, they also recognize individual and communal gifts and skills and invite others to decide how they will participate in God's mission.

Functionally, the keystone species is the catalyst for many elements in the life of a faith community. Through a fourfold cycle, this keystone species supports and directs efforts in a community of faith as it 1) remembers, re-tells, and lives the story of Jesus Christ; 2) invites others to embrace Jesus' way; 3) engages in sustained critical conversations connecting personal stories with God's story; and 4) catalyzes individual and collective action, thus adding their lives and contributions to the story. The explicit and implicit goal is to ensure components of the ecological framework are oriented for equilibrium and co-evolution. In vital and healthy communities, this does not mean that a member of the keystone species "does everything." Instead, they spur collaboration that fosters God's reign.

Pastoral leaders can use an ecology of faith as a framework to identify and evaluate the symbiotic factors that influence efforts to inform, form, and transform the uninitiated and community members. This framework can help leaders to see—both figuratively and literally—not only what is happening within the church's ecosystem, but also how roles and relationships within church communities influence and are influenced by the matrix of elements within the larger universe. Negatively, an ecological perspective reveals how paradigmatic entrenchments can cause "unintended blindness" leading to missed revelation, disintegration of relationships, and dissolution of a community of faith. Positively, the ecological perspective illuminates paradigmatic differences that can provide the necessary crisis for new insights and communal evolution.

THE SIGNIFICANCE OF THE ECOLOGY

An ecological understanding reveals the interdependent components that form people, particularly in faith, through a web of relationships (interpersonal, social, cultural, economic, political, and religious). It also illuminates paradigms operative within and across them and highlights their role as maps and mapmaking tools that can both aid and restrict insight and understanding. These variables moderate the state of an equilibrium-seeking ecosystem through states of *growth, stability,* or *decline.* The combination of systemic components (collection, creed, code, cultus, and community), personal characteristics (commitments to God, self, the community, and creation), and communal features (paradigmatic orientation, diversity, and locality) highlight the multi-variant elements of an ecology of faith. This schema also recognizes the key roles of sustained critical interaction and the keystone species.

These components present a complex integration of elements that inform, form, and transform individuals and communities. Using this framework, evangelization and formation ministries clearly are embedded in the life of a faith community: personally through intentional, sustained, critical dialogue and mutual relationships, as well as corporately, through interactive, holistic, multi-modal, and multi-sensory processes of proclamation, teaching, prayer, worship, and service. By creating opportunities for members to engage one another and the community's primary sources and resources, members are shaped by the community's stories, signs, meanings, and values, and in turn fashion others. Grounded by a vision of God's reign, the circle of conversion and cycle of discipleship recognize the interdependence among personal conversion, social responsibility, and communal justice, and call members to respond such that they contribute to the transformation of the world.

This vision of how the faith is passed from one generation to the next presumes that the faith community regularly gathers in physical contexts to keep, share, and make new God's story. The challenges of decreasing religious literacy and increasing demands are complicating faith communities' efforts. The twenty-first century is increasingly a post-denominational, post-congregational context. With two thousand years of adapting to new contexts, Christians are again becoming nomads seeking new ways to proclaim the gospel and make Christians. By using an ecological perspective and following the mantra "Message, Method, then Media," pastoral leaders can embrace the unique contributions of digital media and social networking.

🕮 further reflection

- Recall the elements that formed you in faith. Write down salient moments and experiences. What do you notice about them?
- During the 1950s, the peak season of denominational growth, the American culture's Protestant ethos and social norms significantly contributed to faith community efforts to proclaim the gospel and make Christians. Can you identify ways that Christianity was embedded in and communicated by secular institutions then? Now?

- Today, the ecology of faith that supplemented what occurred within a faith community with Christian messages from the environment that surrounded it is broken. Has your faith community continued to operate as if it still exists? What have you changed?
- Can you identify elements of growth, stability, or decline in your faith community using the systemic, personal, and communal elements of an ecology of faith? What does your community offer to people who participate in it? What does your community ask from participants and practitioners?
- Can you identify the formal and informal members of the keystone species in your faith community? How are they contributing to your community's stability, growth, or decline?
- If we are formed and shaped by all the elements in our environment, consciously and unconsciously, implicitly and explicitly, how is your community managing the complexity?

Continue the conversation online at
http://faithformation4-0.com.

→ 7

Message, Method, *then* Media

For there is no distinction between Jew and Greek; the same LORD is LORD of all and is generous to all who call on him. For, "Everyone who calls on the name of the LORD shall be saved." But how are they to call on one in whom they have not believed? And how are they to believe in one of whom they have never heard? And how are they to hear without someone to proclaim him? And how are they to proclaim him unless they are sent? Romans 10:12–15

In addition to the media that dominated previous eras, the interactive age provides an expansive array of digital media and social networking to connect people and communicate information and ideas. In any given minute, 571 new websites are created, WordPress users publish 347 new blog posts, the mobile web receives 217 new users, YouTube users upload 48 hours of new video, e-mail users send 204,166,667 messages, Google receives over 2,000,000 search inquiries, consumers spend $272,020 on web shopping, Twitter users send over 100,000 tweets, Apple receives about 47,000 app downloads, brands and organizations receive 34,722 "likes" on

Facebook, Flickr users add 3,125 new photos, and Foursquare users perform 2,083 check-ins.[1]

In this cacophony, businesses and individuals are experimenting with various formats to determine the best methods to attract attention and proclaim their message. Most stories on the nightly news now end with the anchor encouraging viewers to "follow" the station on Twitter and share home videos of breaking news on the station's website. Movie previews at the cineplex provide URLs for viewers to find out more about the cast and production process, and feature films are expanding markets by simultaneously releasing streaming media and DVD versions with extra scenes and "the making of" stories. Increasingly, newspapers and novels are weaving paper-based story lines with digital ones hoping to catch the "eyeballs" of the United States' 239,893,600 Internet users.[2] Even this book has a companion website (*http://faithformation4-0.com*) to post relevant links and current developments as well as encourage sustained critical dialogue. With 80 percent of the United States population online, it feels as if *everyone* and *everything* is moving online.

Within this digital context, it is no surprise that faith communities are considering ways to incorporate the Internet and Web 2.0 tools in their evangelization and formation toolkits. As a newly ordained priest, the Reverend Matthew Moretz created a video blog, *Father Matthew's V-blog*, which was launched on August 16, 2006, as he began his ministry to replant St. Paul's Church in Yonkers, New York. It has evolved into a very popular YouTube series, *Father Matthew Presents,* that offers one- to three-minute videos about Jesus,

---

1. This list is from a graphic, "How Much Data is Created Every Minute?," posted on June 8, 2012, by Josh James, founder, CEO, and chairman of the board of Domo, a technology company focused on business intelligence, *http://www.domo.com/blog/2012/06/how-much-data-is-created-every-minute*. The glossary includes definitions for these and other forms of digital media and social networking.

2. 28,810,937 people between 2000 and 2010, an increase from 281,421,906 to 310,232,863. The total population with Internet added 115,893,600 people, an increase from 124,000,000 to 239,893,600, a move from 44.1 percent to 77.3 percent of the total population.

the Bible, and Christianity in general, and The Episcopal Church in particular. Intended for people who are unfamiliar with the church and are just beginning to gain religious literacy, the videos introduce a wide spectrum of foundational themes in a fun, lighthearted way with Father Matthew's puppet friends Regina and Jehosephat, his dog Beauregard, and a variety of other guests.

Videos and other evangelization and formation resources like Father Matthew's are available almost anywhere at almost any time on desktop and laptop computers as well as mobile devices including cell phones, iPads, and tablets. Christian communities have a long history of "trying on" new methods for communicating and adapting to new cultural conditions. Consider the shifts as the stories Jesus' followers told about his life and work were recorded by scribes, carved into stone, painted on canvases, and broadcast through print and electronic mass media. Today, digital media and social networking are inspiring similar paradigm shifting changes. One of the greatest challenges as pastoral leaders navigate this shift is determining how to choose from the variety of media options available. Related are knowing when a mediated solution is warranted and how to integrate media in a manner sensitive to and aware of the whole ecology of faith.

In previous decades, Christian values were communicated by a variety of institutions in the United States—prayer in public schools, Christmas crèches in front of government buildings, denominationally produced radio and television programs aired in primetime. This environment encouraged and enabled faith communities to concentrate their efforts to proclaim the gospel and make Christians through Sunday morning worship services and educational offerings. This model of church is no longer effective. The wider culture is recognizing its diversity and changing social customs as it acknowledges other faith groups and personal practices. Today, local faith communities are the primary—and often only—medium of evangelization and faith formation. Minimally, Sunday morning activities need augmentation to reach people both within and outside faith communities; ideally creative alternatives and bold visions need consideration.

Many people of faith and religious organizations are using digital media and social networking in the hope of reaching the spectrum of people on the cycle of discipleship. Some examples of their evangelization and formation efforts include:

- *24-7 Prayer* is an international, interdenominational movement of prayer, mission, and justice. The website helps individuals organize local activities, displays tweets of prayer locations and prayer requests, and sponsors a prayer wall. *http://24-7prayer.com*
- *WordLive* is a free, online resource offering daily readings and alternative visual expressions for meeting God through the Bible. *http://www.wordlive.org*
- *SacredSpace* is a multi-language daily prayer online site from the Irish Province of the Society of Jesus (the Jesuits). *http://www.sacredspace.ie*
- *Foundations21* is a free online discipleship resource designed to help individuals and communities grow in Christian faith and witness. *http://www.foundations21.net*
- *Faith Formation Learning Exchange* is an extensive collection of current information, research, and resources for faith formation across the lifespan sponsored by Vibrant Faith Ministries. *http://www.faithformationlearningexchange.net*
- *Center for Spiritual Resources* is a program, resource, and connection clearinghouse sponsored by the Center for Spiritual Resources, Cathedral of All Souls, the Episcopal Diocese of Western NC, and Virginia Theological Seminary's Center for the Ministry of Teaching. *http://thecsr.org*
- *FaithVillage* is a social network for faith experiences where digital participants can set up a loft, meet new friends, engage in discussion and debate, study Scripture, watch inspiring videos, and join causes. *http://faithvillage.com*
- *Trinity Institute* is an annual simulcast interactive web conference shared by global sites hosted by Trinity Wall Street, an Episcopal

church as well as an extensive digital presence. *http://www.trinity wallstreet.org*

- *Education for Ministry Online* is the online version of a successful adult formation process that includes study, prayer, and reflection with six to twelve participants. *http://www.sewanee.edu/EFM/ EFMONLINE.htm*
- *OnceCatholic* is the Franciscan Media interactive ministry to disenfranchised Roman Catholics. *http://oncecatholic.org*
- *Anglicans of Second Life* is a virtual Christian community established in 2007 that follows the Episcopal/Anglican tradition in Second Life, a virtual world created through gaming technology. *http://slangcath.wordpress.com*
- *Art/y/fact.Xn* is a mobile app for interpreting and meditating with Christian art. *http://itunes.apple.com/us/app/art-y-fact.xn/ id480642369?mt =8*
- *Confession: A Roman Catholic App* is a tool to prayerfully prepare for and participate in the Rite of Penance. *http://itunes.apple.com/ us/app/confession-roman-catholic/id416019676?mt=8*

This illustrative list highlights the breadth of creativity and depth of personal and organizational commitments, as faithful people, faith communities, and religious institutions learn to integrate digital media and social networking in formal and informal evangelization and formation efforts. Some developers are feeling successful as growing populations find and use their resources while others lament limited use. The reason some applications succeed and others flounder is not always clear. One caution is to avoid using a new technology that may not be appropriate for an intended outcome.

Faith communities and religious organizations that clearly define who they want to reach, what they hope to accomplish, and why it is important before making any media decisions can avoid the hype of a new technology. By thinking strategically, faith communities can align media decisions with the communal context and orienting mission. It is important to remember that each medium—a person as well as print, electronic and digital resources—has embedded strengths and limitations that make it ideal in some evangelization and formational contexts and not in others. Tapping communications and educational theory, faith communities can make a plan using an easy-to-remember mantra—"Message, Method, *then* Media"—to tailor efforts. This will ensure that they incorporate the best techniques and resources to successfully navigate the obstacles that may be hindering seekers as well as longtime members' participation.

DEVELOPING A PLAN

An ecology of faith recognizes a wide assortment of elements that invite seekers and form members within a faith community. These typically include a wide range of opportunities to strengthen one's faith through personal and communal prayer, worship, teaching/learning, guidance, healing, service/outreach, enablement, and advocacy. While many of these elements will be included in every community's evangelization and formation approaches, pastoral leaders need to tailor elements to fit their unique context; what works in one community will not always be replicable in another community.

By asking strategic, direction-setting questions, pastoral leaders can identify communal values and priorities, and develop plans that respond to individual and communal needs and build upon personal and corporate strengths, interests, and passions. Blending education and marketing theories, these questions ask:

• WHO
   • is saying/doing/providing WHAT
   • to/for WHOM
   • at what PLACE/SPACE (WHERE)
   • at what TIME (WHEN)
   • for what PURPOSE (WHY)

- by what AUTHORITY
- for whose BENEFIT/EMPOWERMENT/ PROFIT
- at whose EXPENSE/DISEMPOWERMENT/ COST
- and with what models/techniques/tools for ASSESSMENT/ EVALUATION

Using collected answers, plans can be harmonized with a community's mission and context.

As plans are being developed, evangelization and formation approaches should reflect demographic differences including general characteristics like age, race, gender, or nationality, as well as faith-community-specific ones including where people fall on the circle of conversion and cycle of discipleship. Clearly, approaching someone who has never heard about Jesus Christ or is unfamiliar with the history of God's presence throughout Scripture is going to be very different from interacting with someone well versed in theology who wants to go deeper and explore things like the nuances of Bible translations from Hebrew and Greek to English. Similarly, introducing Christian disciplines and practices like walking a labyrinth or praying the rosary will be different with children and adults. After considering the audience, their context (who), and their mission (why), the next three steps correlate message, method, and media (how).

"Message, Method, *then* Media" is a three-stage process designed to help communities avoid the ever-present potential of letting the "tail wag the dog." In an environment that fosters the development and deployment of a dizzying array of technological innovations, the risk is choosing a popular medium only to realize that it cannot assist the community in meeting its mission. By starting with message, then moving through method and media, faith communities can avoid exerting a lot of time and energy in the wrong direction. Additionally, by defining these elements and asking particular questions about each, faith communities will ensure that what they believe (espoused theology) matches what they do (operative theology) and leads to their intended outcome.

MESSAGE

For most faith communities, the *message* correlates with their mission and delineates personal and communal evangelization and/or formation goals. Depending on whom the community is trying to reach, there may be multiple messages at the same time. Identification as a welcoming community is as important as a community's self-understanding and mission. Welcoming those who have not been formed in faith requires a different finesse from welcoming those who know Christian concepts and language. Determining the balance between instructional and experiential models will also be important.

When religious instruction is prioritized, faith communities typically focus on an intellectual, content-oriented definition of message. Messages grounded in systematic or dogmatic theology generally order Christian faith and beliefs using themes that may include God, creation, Jesus/Christology, the Holy Spirit/pneumatology, doctrine of the Trinity, Revelation, salvation/soteriology, the End Times/eschatology, the church/ ecclesiology, sin and grace, sacraments, and Christian living. This structure is reflected in The Episcopal Church's "An Outline of the Faith" (commonly called the catechism) that includes similar topics in a question/answer form.[3] These often become the structure of religious education curriculums and adult forums.

When operating from an ecological view, faith formation includes process as a message and shifts the focus from knowing about religion to practicing faith. From this perspective, two alternative organizing frameworks for a community's message could be the ecology of faith's collection, creeds, codes, and cultuses or Maria Harris's *koinonia* (community), *didache* (teaching), *leiturgia* (prayer/worship), *kerygma* (priestly listening, prophetic speech, and political advocacy), and *diakonia* (serving/ministering). These encourage a more active, holistic approach with emotional, social, spiritual, and practical elements and recognize ways to both share the message and embody it.

---

3. *The Book of Common Prayer* (New York: Church Publishing, Inc., 1979), 843–62.

Conceptually, it helps us remember that to proclaim the message of God's love requires Christians to love; the content, "God loves," and the process, "loving," are both messages.

When balancing cognitive development and holistic formation, the revised version of Benjamin Bloom's *The Taxonomy of Educational Objectives* can be a helpful guide. Beginning in 1956, Bloom tapped his experience as an educational psychologist at the University of Chicago to create a holistic view of education. He recognized that learning often depended on some preliminary knowledge or ability. He divided learning into three primary domains—*affective* (feeling/heart), *psychomotor* (doing/hand, body), and *cognitive* (knowing/head)—and constructed a hierarchical classification system that orders thinking skills from foundational or lower competencies to advanced or higher ones. Bloom's model has been ubiquitous within educational contexts and many have adapted it. Educator and former student Lorin Anderson partnered with Bloom's partner David Krathwohl and a team of experts to update the model. They shifted nouns to verbs to denote competencies and integrate levels of knowledge with instructional tasks of remembering, understanding, applying, analyzing, evaluating, and creating.

These instructional tasks are useful as guides to differentiate the needs of people on the cycle of discipleship. Remembering (memorizing) the Lord's Prayer, the Apostles' Creed, Gospel passages, and other prayers are part of a community's story-keeping and an important skill for new members of the community. Being able to discuss them and reflect on the relational assumptions and expectations expressed within them is part of the community's story-sharing and the first steps of following Jesus' Way. Deciding to act upon the beliefs embedded in them is a means to participate in the Dream of God, create the "kingdom," and unite with God; this is part of the community's story-making. Movement through the levels from remembering to synthesizing supports the message shift from an emphasis on *knowing* about Christianity to actualizing it by *being a Christian*.

Finally, recalling insights from curriculum theory, the message one plans to communicate (the explicit curriculum) and that is sent (what is designed and used; the operative curriculum) is not always what participants take away after hearing a message (received or learned curriculum). Sometimes how messages are organized (the hidden curriculum), the contexts within which they are shared (the implicit curriculum), and what is not said (the null curriculum) speak loudly as well. Consider the ways two different faith communities celebrate the week from Palm Sunday to Easter. The first emphasizes the cross, Good Friday, Jesus' atonement for human sin, and healing; this communicates the message of Jesus' obedience to God and sacrifice for humankind. The second emphasizes the empty tomb, the Easter Vigil, Jesus' triumph over death and promise of new life, and hope; its message is the Resurrection. A community's theological framework and orienting vision are visible in the choices a community makes. Decisions and actions reflect communal values and priorities. Sometimes faith communities are conscious of their implicit messages. Too often, decision-makers are not aware of them. Faith communities need to be aware that implicit messages speak as powerfully as the explicit ones—sometimes more so. They also need to ask whether or not what they say they believe is actually being communicated by how they practice: is the espoused operative?

METHOD

Method refers to the type of engagement and interaction that is needed and/or desired as part of an evangelization or formation effort. Methodologies can be *formal* (institutionally structured as with a judicatory or school), *non-formal* (locally structured, community based), or *informal* (exploratory, playful, unexpected). They may encourage or restrict interaction (open/closed) and may demand attention at specific times or allow participants to make timing decisions (synchronous/asynchronous). Some methods are designed for an individual while others are corporate (personal/communal) and may be self-directed or leader-imposed. Methods also may encourage passive participation or active involvement and could occur in a short intense burst or extended processes.

As a message is proclaimed and embodied, different methodological choices will influence impact and outcome. Ponder the difference between asking someone to make sandwiches to distribute to the homeless after an outdoor worship service and asking that same person to join the team that meets weekly to reflect on Scripture, learn about the reasons people are homeless and what the community is doing to address homelessness, then interacts with people who are homeless at worship and a meal that follows. Methodologically, each of these examples requires different commitments of time, attention, relational engagement, and risk. The method chosen should reflect the message to convey as well as the goals to accomplish. A variety of methodological sources are available for evangelization and formation. I offer three helpful frameworks.

Schiro's Curriculum Ideologies

Most people rely on how they learned about Jesus, their religious tradition and faith practices as they consider ways to share it, typically replicating the methods of their mentors and unaware of other options. Using curriculum theorist Michael Schiro's curricular ideologies, pastoral leaders can recognize their operative paradigm[4] as well as consider alternatives. He graphically illustrates divergent philosophies and visions of education (and formation) using two perpendicular axes that create quadrants representing four curricular ideologies: Scholar Academic, Social Efficiency, Learner Centered, and Social Reconstruction. These axes differentiate where knowledge originates: subjective reality (experience) or objective reality (reason) and the

---

4. There is a quiz in the appendix of *Curriculum Theory* to assess operative assumptions and identify one's paradigm. *Curriculum Theory: Conflicting Visions and Enduring Concerns* (Los Angeles: Sage, 2008) and *Curriculum for Better Schools: The Great Ideological Debate* (Englewood Cliffs, NJ: Educational Technology Publications, 1978).

means by which knowledge is valued; the source of knowledge (i.e. great scholars or respected theologians) or the use of that knowledge (i.e. a master artesian passing on a skill). They also highlight whether participants are valued as having or lacking something of worth to offer as well as whether the learning process is more internally oriented (personal gain) or externally oriented (social gain). Using these axes as a lens, Schiro demonstrates how each "pole" embodies distinct beliefs about the type of knowledge that should be taught, the inherent nature of learners, the nature of schools, the roles and functions of teachers, and the means for assessing teaching-learning processes. These influence methodological choices.

TABLE 4: Schiro's Ideologies

INTERNAL

SOURCE OF KNOWLEDGE

MISSING SOMETHING OF WORTH — OBJECTIVE REALITY

SCHOLAR ACADEMIC

LEARNER CENTERED

SUBJECTIVE REALITY — HAVE SOMETHING OF WORTH

What is valued
Focus on process

Origin of Knowledge
Focus on Learner

SOCIAL EFFICIENCY

SOCIAL RECONSTRUCTION

USE OF KNOWLEDGE

EXTERNAL

Source: Schiro, *Curriculum for Better Schools*

The goal within the *Scholar Academic* ideology is to help learners develop their reasoning ability so as to understand their world and culture. The underlying assumption is that there is a definable body of accumulated knowledge that a community wants to transmit to students. Teachers are recognized as the masters of subject fields—the sage on the stage—and students are perceived as neophytes waiting to be filled by the teacher's accumulated wisdom. Although many bemoan the "banking-style" methodologies of this model, its story-keeping qualities can be used to prepare wisdom keepers who know and understand the tradition. Great preachers could be classified in this broadcast method of sharing the Word, and we all know the positive impact they have had in our lives. Nor would we discount the value of memorizing ancient prayers and repeating ancient customs.

In the *Social Efficiency* ideology, the goal of learning is to provide students with specific skills and capacities so that they can perform well within their context. The underlying assumption is that learning is a time of preparation so that the learner will become a constructive and contributing member of the community. Preparing groups of people for initiation or reception into a community or to celebrate other sacraments is a common expression of social efficiency methods; so are graded religious education and faith formation classes that offer a sequential process for laying foundations in earlier levels and advanced knowledge and practices in later ones. The communal value of this form is helping a faith community to grow together in a vision and understanding of the Dream of God. Challenges occur when individual needs are widely divergent (i.e., an unchurched person with a senior lifelong faith community member). These are not insurmountable, but do point toward including more particularized attention.

In the *Learner-Centered* ideology, the goal is to stimulate students' natural interests and encourage their growth and development. Teachers are facilitators who create learning opportunities and direct focus so that learners develop meaning-making skills. The underlying assumption is that learning best takes place when students are motivated to actively engage in experiences that allow them to create their own knowledge and understanding of the world in which they operate. Learning is seen as a life-long process and assessment is used to help learners identify areas for further growth. *Godly Play* and *Catechesis of the Good Shepherd* are Montessori-based, learner-centered, faith formation curricula. Learner-centered faith formation methods seek to match individual interests and passions with opportunities to experience God's presence and feel awe in creation. More child-centric, these experiential methods could provide a balance to the typically more rational, objective methods used with adults.

In the *Social Reconstruction* ideology, the goal is to reconstruct society in order to make it a better place to live in. In it, the underlying assumption is that *we can* make the world a better place to live in through practice and preparation. Education, then, focuses on aiding learners in their ability to recognize problems in society, envision a different reality, and act to reconstruct it so that there is justice and a better life for all people. Teachers function as companions who help students commit to a set of social ideals, confront real social crisis, and act to improve themselves and the nature of society. The values and methods embedded in social reconstruction methodologies most closely align with faith formation processes designed to promote and enact the vision of the Dream of God. This ideology promotes more experiential methods like immersion experiences that connect knowledge with responsibility and require more active involvement.

Schiro's curricular ideologies frame methodological questions from a systematic, corporate approach and illuminate the perspective of a curriculum developer. Being aware that each human being engages the world differently is implicit in the discussion of each ideology.

Gardner's Multiple Intelligences

When creating evangelization and formation opportunities for a faith community, one needs to be sensitive to individual differences. First published in 1983 in his book *Frames of Mind*, Howard Gardner's notion of multiple intelligences redefines what it means to be "smart" and calls educators to expand their repertoire of teaching-learning methods. Traditionally, intelligence has been measured by IQ (intelligence quotient), which defines smartness by one's ability (or inability) to think with words—*linguistic intelligence*—or to think with numbers and reasoning—*logical-mathematical intelligence*. Within educational settings, classrooms and teaching-learning methods typically privilege highly articulate and logical people, often missing the wisdom of those who think differently. To recognize the potential of the larger population and broaden the spectrum of what is called intelligence, Gardner added seven additional measures of smartness:

- *visual-spatial intelligence*—picture smart
- *bodily-kinesthetic intelligence*—body smart
- *musical intelligence*—music smart
- *interpersonal intelligence*—people smart
- *intrapersonal intelligence*—self smart
- *naturalist intelligence*—nature smart
- *existentialist intelligence*—ultimate realities smart

Gardner's theory expands the horizon of available teaching-learning tools beyond the conventional methods used in most educational contexts (e.g., lecture, textbooks, writing assignments, formulas, etc.).

More teachers are integrating multiple means to communicate messages and teach lessons. This variety includes music, cooperative learning, art activities, role play, multimedia, field trips, inner reflection, and much more. Fortunately, most faith communities already offer a wide range of processes and practices that engage multiple intelligences. The ecology of faith incorporates each of Garner's nine intelligences through multisensory and multi-modal expression that includes singing and playing instruments, liturgical dance and ritual actions, pictures and prayer cards, public worship and private prayer, reading books and writing icons, contemplating stained glass stories and statues, classroom interaction and meditative retreats, service at the altar, and service in the community.

When choosing methodologies, it is helpful to remember that individuals bring a spectrum of abilities to an experience or activity. Pastoral leaders will want to find approaches that enable these gifts to be honed and developed.

Myers-Briggs Type Indicator

Looking beyond an individual's capacity, there are a host of other personality-driven considerations that pastoral leaders will want to be attentive to as they choose evangelization and formation methodologies. Using Carl Jung's typological categories, Katherine Cook Briggs and her daughter Isabel Briggs Myers developed the Myers-Briggs Type Indicator in 1921 as a tool to assess personality. It identifies four opposing pairs or dichotomies that, when combined, result in sixteen possible personality types. The four dichotomies are: 1) extroversion/introversion, 2) sensing/intuiting, 3) thinking/feeling, and 4) judging/perceiving. Extroversion/introversion contrasts active and reflective engagement. It focuses on attitudes toward the world and engagement with it: outwardly for extroverts and inwardly for introverts. Sensing/intuiting and thinking/feeling are ways of engaging information. Sensing/intuiting contrasts how people rely on facts or their "guts" as interpretive styles. Thinking/feeling contrasts logic and empathy as the primary source of information. Judging/perceiving contrasts those who prefer making decisions with those who prefer staying open to possibilities. It explores how people give structure to life and can explain why some people are always on top of details and deadlines while others seem to serendipitously navigate a course. Each of the four dichotomies can reveal a lot about potential and current community members. Knowing which participants are introverted thinkers and which are extroverted thinkers is helpful in a small group conversation or facilitating a formational event in order to encourage sustained, critical conversations.

In the extroverted/introverted dichotomy, people with a preference for extroversion draw energy from action: they tend to act, then reflect, then act further. Their energy is directed outward towards people and objects. Inactivity leads to a decline in their level of energy and motivation. People whose preference is introversion become less energized as they act: they prefer to reflect, then act, then reflect again. Extroverted thinkers thrive during live interaction whether physically together or online, are energized by it, and tend to dominate it. Even though what they say generally sounds like a finished thought, they are often thinking out loud and are learning what they think and believe as they name it. Their interest is maintained by immediate feedback and they are likely to disappear when they lack a catalyst to spur their thinking. Correspondingly, introverted thinkers function best in the internal world of ideas and reflection; they seek depth and are thought oriented. Their flow is directed inward toward concepts and ideas. They need time out to reflect in order to rebuild energy. Introverted thinkers face challenges in live interactions, particularly when those interactions are monopolized by extroverted thinkers. Many claim that conversations move too fast for them to process new material and respond to it in a timely manner. Needing time to reflect upon and develop their thoughts internally, many people report that they are ready to contribute to a class conversation *after* the live interaction has ended. They thrive when breaks are offered so that they can collect their thoughts and offer them to the class. Pastoral leaders will be challenged to maintain a balance, but everyone gains the wisdom of the whole community when this is achieved.

As these descriptions suggest, there are many overlapping elements to consider when identifying a community's message, method, and media. The most compelling evangelization and formation occur when leaders clearly differentiate elements that align the message with the appropriate method and media.

MEDIA

Media refers to the agent, instrument, or combination of these chosen to express a message. The types of media communities choose for story-keeping, story-telling, and story-making impact the messages sent and received. Some stories are best read as text, with its inherent ability to allow us distance from the message to analyze various aspects and discern a path of action; other stories are enhanced by engaging pictures and the tonal quality of a voice narrating it; still other stories are told best as a documentary combining audio and video to capture an event or describe a situation. Along with the commonly considered technologies of print, radio, television, the Internet, and mobile technologies, other media include a person, a community, an artifact, and a ritual. Each of these media has inherent characteristics that can enhance, nuance, or detract from the message expressed. Some are permanent and fixed while others are temporary and adaptable. Their distribution patterns vary, combining synchronous (live) and asynchronous (on demand) with interpersonal (one-to-one), broadcast (one-to-many), or interactive (many-to-many). They incur costs—financial, time, and skill—can inhibit or enhance non-verbal communications, and can restrict or expand availability and accessibility.

Typically, a number of these characteristic elements are combined in a single medium. A printed page is fairly durable, fixed, relatively inexpensive, and portable. It continuously displays whatever its designer wrote or printed on it for ten cents or less per photocopied page and it can be handed to someone, sent in the mail, or tacked on a bulletin board. It also is geographically bound, able to reach only as far as someone can carry or mail it. In contrast a website is flexible and can be updated or changed at any time, multiple people can create and edit it, and it is accessible almost anywhere and anytime, but distractions are inherent as ads are embedded by Internet service providers and the platform used to access it (browsers, search engines, apps, etc.). Also, there are often hidden costs including website hosting, software to create and maintain it, time to develop, or the cost of hiring a professional.

There are at least five distinguishing characteristic sets to consider when determining the most appropriate mix to supports a faith community's rationale:

- broadcast (mono-directional) or interactive
- synchronous (live/same time) or asynchronous (store/delay access)
- physically gathered (onsite or offsite) or mediated/virtual presence (online)
- open (anyone can participate/view) or secure (restricted/password protected)
- safety and social presence

The first decision is whether the faith community wants to simply *share information* (broadcast) or *to encourage dialogue* between information recipients (interactive). From a media perspective, broadcast-oriented technologies are designed for one-way communication, from a sender to many receivers, while interactive technologies encourage many-to-many communication.

Most church newsletters and websites statically display information, "broadcasting" it to whoever happens to pick up a paper copy or surf to the site. Broadcast media typically provide fairly stable, fixed information including descriptions of the faith community and community life, the congregation's vision or mission, messages about and/or from the pastor(s) and/or leadership, hours of worship services, personal reflections or meditations, and invitations to participate in activities. With the likely exception of e-mail information, they do not invite feedback or encourage a response. In contrast, interactive technologies are designed for interpersonal and communal dialogue and typically encourage community members to create as well as respond to what is said or posted online. They may be one-on-one with two people physically together or connected by telephone, Internet chat, or web conference. Small and large groups may gather onsite at the community's gathering place, offsite at a designated location, or online using threaded discussions, virtual spaces, and enhanced congregational websites. These interactive additions often include opportunities to comment on sermons or minutes from monthly meetings, identify prayer requests, and encourage discussion about theological topics or a community practice.

The next two media decisions consider *when* (same time/different times) and *where* (same place/different places) people gather and become the axes for a *time/place* matrix. There are two options with respect to time. Synchronous technologies assume everyone will be present at the same time; asynchronous technologies enable individuals to participate at different times—when it is convenient to their lives. There are two primary place options: same or different. These can be further differentiated as *onsite*—at the faith community's designated gathering place, usually a church; *offsite*—at other specified locations: a member home, a civic meeting space, etc.; *mediated*—at a common technology-created interaction space typically using the Internet and wireless mobile; and *hybrid*—some combination or blending of onsite, off site, and mediated spaces.

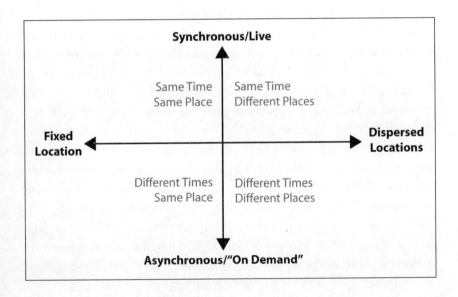

As faith communities determine whom they want to reach and what they want/need to provide for people on the cycle of discipleship, the *time/place matrix* suggests an endless variety of combinations that can acknowledge not only the challenge of finding time to be physically together, but also the diversity of life circumstances. Blending a variety of methods and media can create multiple entry points for individuals and groups to gather that may be centralized, decentralized, or distributed.

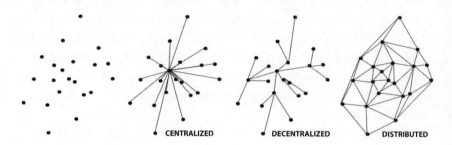

When meeting someone for the first time, it is generally preferable to be physically present at the same time and place. Faith communities that desire live interaction among and between participants and a presenter could schedule a series of educational sessions with everyone gathered at the same place, connected from different places via web conferencing, or interacting with text-based chat and instant messages as well as through avatars in virtual worlds like Second Life. When time is a challenge and interested participants cannot find a commonly agreed upon time, resources could be shared through video or animations with text-based interaction in threaded discussion. Viewed as part of an ecology of faith, this mix moves faith communities from the confines of a physical space to offer evangelization and formation that meets people where they are—literally and figuratively—and invites them to grow through a variety of one-time gatherings (an evening presentation or prayer service), mini-series (four- to six-week Advent or Lent meditations or learning opportunities), day-long or weekend programs (retreats), as well as longer commitments (an immersion experience or service trip, or an academic semester or yearlong course).

Levels of accessibility and security required are the fourth element for faith communities to consider as they decide whether or not and how to share a message. Onsite activities are generally the most open and typically allow anyone present to participate. Offsite locations may be open (gathering at a public place) or closed (gather at a member's home). Online security is generally defined by application settings. Most digital tools enable the site designers to designate whether a website or web tool is available to everyone who finds the site or is restricted to particular members. Social networking sites as well as blogging tools enable users to limit viewers. This is particularly important when moving from a static to an interactive site where there may be privacy concerns such as the use of pictures or discussion of sensitive topics.

Safety and *social presence* are the fifth set of markers for those responsible for making media selection. They indicate a medium's trustworthiness and authenticity when communicating a message as well as a measure of how well a community practices what it preaches. Safety identifies potential issues and concerns faith communities must address when the medium is a person as well as a technology. Social presence offers some strategies for conveying an authentic, "real" self in mediated contexts.

The task when the medium is a person in physically gathered contexts is fairly simple. In addition to visual cues, community members have many means to verify if a person is who they claim to be (friendships between members, contact information, etc.). Religious institutions and faith communities also have developed very detailed policies and protocols[5] for protecting participants from abuse, neglect, or exploitation—particularly guarding children from sexual misconduct. The task is more challenging in mobile and online contexts when unscrupulous individuals create fictitious personas and take advantage of unsuspecting web users who lack live video or other forms of authentication.

---

5. Models include the USCCB Charter for the Protection of Children and Young People, *http:// www.usccb.org/issues-and-action/child-and-youth-protection/charter.cfm*, The Episcopal Church's *Safe guarding God's Children*, *https://www.cpg.org/administrators/insurance/preventing-sexual-misconduct/ overview*, and the Presbyterian Church's *Creating Safe Churches*, *http://www.presbyterianmission. org/ministries/creating-safe-ministries/statements/*

Safety concerns also arise from the nature of digital media. Some are intentional: half truths, lies, and innuendos are as easy to post as the truth, and once sent or posted, digital information is public and available for copy, manipulation, and redistribution. Others may be unintentional: text messages can be misinterpreted and cause hurt when physical presence and non-verbal reinforcement of tone and meaning are missing. Digital media and social networking are difficult to control but individuals and communities can decide whether or not and how to incorporate them and develop methods to monitor and reinforce their appropriate use. Fortunately, many religious institutions, denominations, and faith communities are leading the way by developing use policies to direct media choices and ensure safety.[6]

A faith community's ability to recognize and promote *social presence* in digital environments also is a way to ensure authenticity and healthy relationships. Its nuanced meanings[7] have evolved to describe a medium's ability to convey a sense of "being there" as if physically present, and to support social and emotional engagement between participants using a medium. Early research evaluating a medium's potential to replicate "real" interaction was positive, highlighting the intimacy of

---

6. The Episcopal Diocese of Connecticut had one of the first and most comprehensive documents, "Suggested practices and guidelines for use of social networking websites and other forms of digital communication," *http://www.ctdiocese.org/images/customer-files//SocialMediaGuidelinesbooklet.pdf*. Justin Wise, the executive director for the Center for Church Communications, created "The Ultimate List of Social Media Policies for Churches and Ministries," *http://justinwise.net/social-media-policies-churches-ministries*. The Kentucky Baptist Convention offers a "Sample Internet Usage Policy" at *http://web.kybaptist.org/web/doc/InternetUsePolicy.pdf*. The United States Conference of Catholic Bishops developed "Social Media Guidelines," *http://www.usccb.org/about/communications/social-media-guidelines.cfm* and recommendations for "Using New Media in the New Evangelization," *http://www.usccb.org/about/leadership/usccb-general-assembly/2012-june-meeting/using-the-new-media-for-the-new-evangelization.cfm*. Mark Vitalis Hoffman, a professor at Lutheran Theological Seminary at Gettysburg, offers a collection of "Guides and Guidelines for a Church Website" at *http://www.gettysburgseminary.org/mhoffman/xnlinks/pomschurchweb08.htm*. St. Margaret Mary Catholic Church offers "Video and Webcasting Policies and Guidelines" at *http://www.stmargaretmary.org/videoweb castingpolicy.pdf*.

7. Social presence is defined as the degree to which people are *perceived* as "real" in CMC (Gunawardena, 1995), the ability of students "to *project* themselves socially and emotionally as 'real' people" (Garrison et al., 2000, 94); the degree of feeling, perception, and reaction of being connected by CMC to another person (Tu and McIsaac, 2002); and students' perceptions of being in and belonging in an online course (Picciano, 2002).

telephone communications. Computers left a more negative evaluation as a task-centric, isolating medium. The addition of network capability and social media applications reveal more positive results.

Canadian educators D. Randy Garrison, Terry Anderson, and Walter Archer evaluated social presence in online education in a way that may be helpful for faith communities considering digital media and social networking options for evangelization and formation. Like faith communities engaged in sustained critical interaction, they assume that communities create and re-create experiences and knowledge through the critical analysis of subject matter, questioning, and the challenging of assumptions. They define social presence as the ability of participants to project themselves socially and emotionally as "real" people in those conversations through the medium of communication being used. One of the ways offered as a measure of "real" presence that faith communities could appropriate is an awareness of the manner in which social expressions are included in an digital conversation: the way participants addressed each other by name, offered complements, expressed appreciation, commented on one another's responses, expressed emotion, used humor, and said goodbye.

In addition to these major elements, faith communities also need to be aware of other factors as they consider media choices. Do community members have the resources (equipment, software, bandwidth, personnel, etc.), technical proficiency, and audience awareness to create and maintain the type of resources they want to provide? Are there access issues (individually and communally) including economics that impact investment in digital technologies, network availability to distribute a message, and physical abilities like visual impairments? Similarly, are there concerns about sharing a community's intellectual property or crossing the boundaries of copyright law?

IMPLEMENTATION AND EVALUATION

The digital age provides both challenges and opportunities as faith communities experience paradigm-shifting change. The population of American adults who claim no religious affiliation is growing, and trusted models to proclaim the gospel and make Christians are failing. Many faith communities and religious organizations are tapping digital media and social networking to offer people both within and outside our communities access to spiritual and religious resources. By asking strategic, direction-setting questions, pastoral leaders can ensure that evangelization and formation approaches match communal values and priorities. By ordering planning using the mantra "message, method, then media," we can appropriately incorporate new technologies within existing patterns and processes that respond to individual and communal needs and build upon personal and corporate strengths, interests, and passions. As plans are enacted, particularly after initiatives conclude, there needs to be a review of what worked and what did not. This final stage is often forgotten under the weight of other deadlines and programs, but it is likely the most critical. Plans are made with a set of assumptions about the faith community, the effort's particular audience, and the team putting it into place. Revisiting the original elements—who is saying/doing/providing what to/for whom, at what place/space (where), at what time (when), for what purpose (why), by what authority, for whose benefit/profit/empowerment, and at whose expense/cost/disempowerment—with an awareness of the circle of conversion, the cycle of discipleship, and an ecology of faith will ensure necessary revisions occur.

✪ further reflection

- What have you learned about inviting seekers and forming members in this chapter?
- Does your faith community have a plan to ensure that seekers and members know the stories of God's action throughout history? Can you articulate your community's mission and vision? Do your practices match what you espouse?

- Can you identify the message, method, and media you are currently using and/or would like to use? Can you identify the strengths and limitations of various methods and media? Will this information influence your efforts?

- For most of the past century, evangelization and formation efforts typically have occurred within the physical walls of church buildings. Where does your community host its events? How are they or can they be integrated into your ecology of faith?

- Can you imagine ways of using digital media and social networking to augment or replace aspects of your evangelization and faith formation efforts? How would you describe their potential benefits and limitations in your community? Do you think social media can provide a forum for an authentic Christian community? Can it inspire personal conversion and social transformation?

Continue the conversation online at
http://faithformation4-0.com.

→8

Following The Way in the Digital Age

Then an angel of the LORD said to Philip, "Get up and go toward the south to the road that goes down from Jerusalem to Gaza." (This is a wilderness road.) So he got up and went. Now there was an Ethiopian eunuch, a court official of the Candace, queen of the Ethiopians, in charge of her entire treasury. He had come to Jerusalem to worship and was returning home; seated in his chariot, he was reading the prophet Isaiah. Then the Spirit said to Philip, "Go over to this chariot and join it." So Philip ran up to it and heard him reading the prophet Isaiah. He asked, "Do you understand what you are reading?" He replied, "How can I, unless someone guides me?" And he invited Philip to get in and sit beside him. Now the passage of the scripture that he was reading was this: "Like a sheep he was led to the slaughter, and like a lamb silent before its shearer, so he does not open his mouth. In his humiliation justice was denied him. Who can describe his generation? For his life is taken away from the earth." The eunuch asked Philip, "About whom, may I ask you, does the prophet say this, about himself or about someone else?"

continued

> Then Philip began to speak, and starting with this scripture, he proclaimed to him the good news about Jesus. As they were going along the road, they came to some water; and the eunuch said, "Look, here is water! What is to prevent me from being baptized?" He commanded the chariot to stop, and both of them, Philip and the eunuch, went down into the water, and Philip baptized him. When they came up out of the water, the Spirit of the LORD snatched Philip away; the eunuch saw him no more, and went on his way rejoicing. But Philip found himself at Azotus, and as he was passing through the region, he proclaimed the good news to all the towns until he came to Caesarea. Acts 8:26–40

The story of the Ethiopian eunuch tells us a lot about evangelization and formation. Although the account does not have Philip saying much, his actions demonstrate his confidence in God's direction. Spurred by an angel of the Lord, he left Samaria on a deserted road in the middle of the day. He was likely surprised when a chariot appeared and even more so by the sight of an Ethiopian court official reading Scripture; the ability to read and to have a written text was rare. Unflinching, Philip followed the Spirit's direction, running to the chariot and initiating a conversation about the readings. The eunuch's question, "How can I (understand) unless someone guides me?" is telling. Unfamiliar with the story of Jesus and unable to interpret the words' meaning, the eunuch admitted his limitations—despite his office and presumed wealth—and vulnerably asked for help. With the authority of a story-keeper—someone well familiar with the passage and its relationship to Jesus—Philip led a story-sharing process that inspired the eunuch to take the message of the gospel into his heart and to ask to be baptized. The gospel story ends with the Ethiopian eunuch going on his way rejoicing, but we learn in Eusebius's

Historia Ecclesiastica[1] that it is really a new story's beginning. The newly initiated Ethiopian eunuch returned to his homeland and became an evangelist.

On the surface, this story offers an example of how Jesus' followers, trusting God's action in their lives, inspire others through the circle of conversion. Relational openness enabled Philip and the Ethiopian eunuch to enter into genuine dialog and share a journey that resulted in the eunuch's conversion. A cycle of discipleship is implicit as Philip modeled leadership and mentored the eunuch in such a way that the eunuch was inspired and empowered to do the same. They each somehow understood that they were responsible for knowing, keeping, sharing, and adding to the story. In addition to explicitly modeling a process of evangelization and formation, Luke, the author of the Acts of the Apostles, implicitly reminds his readers of Jesus' commission to "*Go into all the world and proclaim the good news to the whole creation*" (Mark 16:15).

The story begins in Samaria where Philip's ministry was already taking the gospel beyond its original Jewish audience. The animosity between Jews and Samaritans is well documented, but they at least shared belief in the same God. By including Philip's journey with the Ethiopia eunuch, Luke stretched the borders of who could (should) be included in the disciples' mission even further. Ethiopia literally was the end of the earth in the ancient world and its people were Gentiles. Philip and the Ethiopian's relationship meant that the good news reached new geographic and ethnic limits. Moreover, the eunuch likely had a physical deformity that would prohibit entry into the temple (Deuteronomy 23:1). The term "eunuch" is used in the Septuagint to refer to either a high official or to a castrated male. Because Luke also clearly identified the man as a court official, he probably used the term to indicate the eunuch was emasculated. Thus, the story also emphasizes the Christian concern for those who find themselves outside of the religious mainstream. Explicitly and

1. Eusebius, *Historia Ecclesiastica*, 2.2, 13–14.

implicitly, the central message of Luke's story is a call to remove *any* barrier that excludes.

CALLED TO BE LIKE PHILIP

By baptism, all Christians are called to be like Philip. We are asked to trust in the Lord, to listen to the Spirit whispering in our ears, and to respond. We are challenged to look outside the doors of our hearts and church structures to welcome and embrace *all*—regardless of difference. We are asked to establish pathways not only to proclaim the good news but also to ensure that those who hear it can understand it. This vision presumes that the collected stories, creedal beliefs, cultic practices, and behavior codes of a community are accessible along with story-keepers to share and interpret them.

Successful implementation of this vision is a growing challenge for many faith communities. Significant portions of the general population no longer know or understand Christian stories, traditions, and practices, and the number of people who feel confident interpreting them for others is decreasing. There is a growing gap between those who are active church members and the rest of society. One in five adults in the United States does not claim a church affiliation either because they were never part of a church or because they have become disenfranchised from religious organizations. This population is increasing generationally as one in three adults in the United States under the age of thirty currently identifies as unaffiliated. The situation becomes more complex when, as described in chapter six, many of those who are committed to a faith community find it difficult or impossible to be active in their church. Increasingly, individuals find little opportunity to gather physically to engage in genuine dialog and sustained critical interaction.

Fortunately, digital media and social networking are a gift that can enable faith communities to be creative in how they structure and restructure models of evangelization and formation. Providing options for how, when, and where activities occur can remove barriers that prohibit a community's story-keeping, story-sharing, and story-making efforts. Distributed models of sustained critical interaction and resource sharing can provide access and are increasingly becoming the norm as communities reimagine ways to connect with people both within and outside their community. Distributed leadership is also emerging in this networked environment to tap the wisdom of the whole community.

RESOURCE SHARING

An ecology of faith has always embraced distributed models in which evangelization and formation, as well as the leaders designing and enacting them, are available from a variety of access points in an ecosystem. Through four eras of communication, pastoral leaders adapted their methods of proclaiming the gospel and making Christians to meet contemporary needs and utilize emerging technologies. In the mid-twentieth century, Christian messages proclaimed during Sunday worship, taught during Sunday School and adult education forums, and enacted through service and outreach were reinforced, implicitly and explicitly, by an American civil religion practiced in governmental institutions, taught in the public schools, and broadcast through print and electronic media. Today, we are in a new context as faith communities become the primary—if not only—source of Christian story-keeping, story-sharing, and story-making.

The twenty-first century is in the midst of significant paradigm shifts, particularly as new methods and media supplement and supplant older ones. Faith communities that have typically been more internally focused on communal worship and faith formation are experiencing a decrease in community rosters and the subsequent decline of resources. Rather than focus inwardly on scarcity, faithful people need to turn outward and take the story of Philip and the Ethiopian eunuch to heart. This shift requires trust in God, and a reorientation of efforts to ensure that all God's people have access to the communities' collected stories and traditions, creedal beliefs, behavioral codes, and cultic rituals.

By boldly re-imagining ways to be in relationship utilizing digital media and social networking, faith communities can establish new methods to invite seekers and engage faithful members. By asking what *must* be done physically together and what *could* be done online, faithful people can develop new ways to sustain critical interaction and cultivate faith. As many congregations and denominations are learning, there are many aspects of communal life that can be augmented by digital media and social networking to provide a sense of "being there." This was evident at The Episcopal Church's recent convention.

All sorts of digital technologies—desktops, laptops, netbooks, personal digital assistants (PDAs), tablets, cell phones, etc.—helped to reinforce the participatory nature of The Episcopal Church's polity, particularly during its 77th General Convention. Though I was in my hotel room across the street from the Indianapolis Convention Center working on this manuscript, I simultaneously followed the discussion and debate (along with a fair mix of humor) in *both* the House of Deputies and the House of Bishops through Livestream, a live audio and video signal broadcast from the convention center floor. The abundance of digital activity was not limited to the legislative floor. The Episcopal Church's media hub (*http://episcopaldigital network.com/gc2012*) gave access to the songs, readings, and sermons of daily worship along with interviews, updated schedules, revised resolutions, and deputy handbooks. The General Convention Twitter feed (#GC77) was active with a rolling list of current tweets that included comments on legislation, announcements about initiatives like the Acts 8 flash mob, and prayer for Jerry Lamb, provisional bishop of the Diocese of San Joaquin who had suffered two minor strokes. The Episcopal News Service (ENS) was actively posting news releases and a group of deputies tapped experts outside the convention to craft an amendment to a resolution using a Google hangout—a multi-person web conferencing and desktop collaboration space. These mediated expressions were available to me in my room as well as anyone worldwide who accessed the signal using some form of web-enabled computer or mobile device.

Many faith communities are also effectively incorporating digital media and social networking in their evangelization and faith formation toolkits. The traditional pastoral care home visit and telephone call is augmented with check-ins via Facebook's live instant messaging and stored wall posts. Educational conversations previously restricted to the parish hall are being offered live through web conferencing services like Adobe Connect and WebEx as well as recorded for future viewing on YouTube and Vimeo. Even sermons and worship services are available live through audio and video streaming or archived using services like Ustream. These exemplary efforts creatively capitalize on the inherent characteristics of various media to enable community members' full, active, and conscious participation. They are distributed points of evangelization and faith formation that, when combined, maintain a vital ecology of faith.

The primary focus of this book has been to provide a comprehensive process to make decisions about whether and how to use media for evangelization and formation. This is a vision of a distributed network for sustained critical interaction and resource sharing. It requires a shift from a central point of origination for a community's evangelization and faith formation to include a variety of other places and virtual spaces. More than any one person can (or should) try to develop and offer, it also includes a parallel shift from a more hierarchical structure to a distributed model of leadership.

DISTRIBUTED LEADERSHIP

One of the greatest changes occurring as faith communities shift from a more broadcast method of evangelization and faith formation to a more interactive one is the parallel change in understanding of leadership. Faith formation 3.0 typically defined leadership from a programmatic perspective and typically hired an individual as the leader responsible for making things happen. Although many larger communities could afford a team that collaboratively shared leader functions, the majority of faith communities only have financial resources to hire one church professional, and that typically is an ordained priest. In this model, the professional was often placed in an untenable situation of being asked to be responsible for everything that occurs within a faith community, regardless of training or ability to do so. Sometimes church professionals fostered this style of leadership; more often it was presumed by community members to justify the community's economic investment in a salary. Communal expectations of church professionals also expanded as increasing work, family, and other expectations led community members to eliminate what they understood as "voluntary" commitments. Many congregations are recognizing that hierarchical models are not always healthy for a community or its paid professionals. Faith formation 4.0 enables a shift to embrace shared models of ministry and utilize distributive models of leadership.

Marshall Ganz defines leadership as "accepting responsibility for enabling others to achieve purpose in the face of uncertainty." Leadership in this model is not a position that one holds but decisions one makes to take action. By baptism, every member of the faith community is called to leadership. As part of the Body of Christ, everyone is asked to make decisions that enact the Dream of God. In the ideal, every member is recognized for his or her unique gifts and resources and offers them to the common good. By sharing talents, everyone contributes to the vitality of the faith community as well as the larger world. In an ecological model, decisions and actions are facilitated by the keystone species—a group whose presence is crucial to the community's survival. Rather than be responsible for doing everything within communal life, the keystone species fosters stability and growth by both orienting activity within God's mission and guiding others toward communal action to serve that mission.

Ultimately, within a Christian community of faith, the keystone species is God as revealed through Jesus Christ and the Holy Spirit.

Functionally, the keystone species are church professionals and community members who empower others to share their gifts and the responsibility for proclaiming the gospel and making Christians. The keystone species—paid and unpaid—animate the community's story-keeping, story-sharing, and story-making. They know the stories of God's loving presence throughout history, help us to claim and proclaim God's promise of life abundant, and challenge us to put faith into action, thus adding our stories to the wisdom of the ages. Along the way, they fertilize our faith by coordinating opportunities for spiritual practice, offering resources to help us interpret the things that we see and hear, and providing seeds for fruit that we may not have known existed. Together we reach toward the Dream of God.

REACHING THE DREAM

Reaching toward the Dream of God looks different in each passing decade. The late-twentieth-century introduction of interactive media has sparked much discussion and debate. With the move to embrace digital media and social networking for evangelization and formation, many are asking if traditional media are obsolete. I don't think so. Humans still communicate orally, in writing, with art and artifacts, and through mass mediated print and electronic media. In most contexts, these traditional media are still being produced in their original form, and augmented for distribution through new digital venues. Books are still text-based manuscripts, the majority of which are printed on paper and published for mass market consumption. According to the September 2012 Aptara Survey of Publishing Professionals report, "Revealing the Business of eBooks," while 80 percent of publishers are now producing eBooks, only 10 percent of current publishers plan to produce eBooks *instead* of paper versions and 16 percent have *no plans* to produce eBooks. There is no doubt that voice, video, and data are converging in digital forms and access will increasingly be through mobile and other networked media; still, traditional media will be present—at least for a bit more time. The reason: full digital media and social integration will require a *generational shift.*

The Pew Internet and American Life Project[2] has published data about the impact of the digital age since its first report in March 2000. Their studies reveal that since 2006, the number of American adults who can go online has remained fairly stable at 79 percent. Of all those with Internet access, roughly one in six adults does not *use* the Internet and a majority of adults—seven of ten—are "overwhelmed by the amount of news and information available today." The main reasons 21 percent of the American population does not go online are lack of interest (31 percent), lack of access (12 percent said no computer), expense (10 percent), and difficulty of use (9 percent). Traditional media are relatively secure today—but change is coming. The 2010 comparison of social networking use by generation shows 16 percent of the GI Generation (74+), 34 percent of the Silent Generation (65–73), 43 percent of older Boomers (55–64), 50 percent of younger Boomers (45–55), 62 percent of Gen Xers (34–45), and 83 percent of Millennial (18–33). The full impact of digital media and social networking will be realized when Gen X and the Millennials, along with those who follow them, represent the majority of the population. We need to plan for the present, with the future in mind. This will take time and patience.

Not long after my niece Maggie, the third of my brother and sister-in-law's children, was born, Bill and Sharon knew they were outgrowing their "starter" home and began planning for the next stage of their lives together. One afternoon, Bill came home excited about a piece of property he found that overlooked Seven Valleys, a beautiful area of cascading hills in southeastern Pennsylvania. Over the

2. Information has been compiled from a number of Pew Internet and American Life Project reports: *Generations 2010, http://www.pewinternet.org/Reports/2010/Generations-2010/Introduction/ Generations-online-and-offline.aspx; Reaching Your Audience in the Digital Age: Key Research Trends to Watch,* September 2, 2012, Aaron Smith, Research Associate, *http://pewinternet.org/Presentations/ 2012/Sep/Reaching-Your-Audience-in-the-Digital-Age.aspx*

next few weeks, he and Sharon visited the property and came to love the breathtaking sunsets they saw from its vista. They could imagine a place to position a house to take advantage of the panorama, the garden for homegrown vegetables, a jungle gym for the kids, and a pool for family and friends to gather. As a young couple, they were not in the position to immediately make their dream a reality. Still, they got a loan to purchase the property and began to develop plans. For the next two years, they went to open houses and searched catalogues until they were satisfied with the list of elements they wanted to include. Over the next year, they worked out details with the bank and had a builder construct the core elements, finishing what they needed right away—the main floor and bedrooms—leaving other areas to be completed over time. When they moved in, the space above the garage had electricity but was waiting for sheetrock and trim to make it a guest room, and the unfinished basement had all the preliminary stages for a future fireplace, bathroom, living area, and workroom. Over the last eleven years, Bill and Sharon completed different aspects of the dream. A few fruit trees and garden areas came first. The room I use when I visit a few years later. More recently, the pool was completed so that their now-teenaged children have a safe and welcoming place for their friends. It could not happen all at once, but it oriented their priorities and decisions as they considered vacation plans and holiday gift-giving. There were a few adjustments along the way, especially as new methods and materials emerged. With time and intention, the dream was fulfilled.

Preparing for and enacting the Dream of God occurs in much the same way. Jesus gave us a vision of life greater than we can imagine and told us that it is both already and not yet present. The community that follows his Way has kept the dream alive, adapting methods and media to meet contemporary needs and contexts. The digital age and its distributed forms of evangelization, faith formation, and leadership move us to a more collaborative model and hopefully another step closer to the reality God offers.

🙂 further reflection

- The story of Philip and the Ethiopian eunuch illustrates aspects of evangelization and faith formation. Which speaks to you and your community? What elements do you see operative in your community? What needs to be strengthened?

- The digital age is prompting many communities to restructure their evangelization and faith formation efforts to encourage distributed interaction and resource sharing. Is this happening in your faith community? How can it be strengthened?

- The digital age also is a catalyst for an organizational shift that defines leadership as "accepting responsibility for enabling others to achieve purpose in the face of uncertainty." Rather than a hierarchical structure that puts all the responsibility for God's mission on church professionals, this encourages a distributed model where all are called to share their gifts and resources with the wider community. Is this happening in your faith community? How can it be strengthened?

- Enacting the Dream of God requires a shared vision and time to implement it. How do you and your community imagine the Dream of God? How are you moving to enact it? Are your evangelization and faith formation oriented toward it?

- So what? Jane E. Regan, Boston College associate professor of theology and religious education, asks "So what?" to test meaningfulness. Now that you have read the book and discussed the questions, what difference will this manuscript have on you? Your community? Your efforts to proclaim the gospel and make Christians?

 Continue the conversation online at
http://faithformation4-0.com.

glossary

adherent: A person who identifies with and claims a religious tradition. It is a broader term than "member," which typically has a technical definition and refers to an official status that varies according to congregation or denomination.

agnostics: Skeptics who claim it is impossible to know if there is a God but do not profess atheism. (These people make up 2.4 percent of the U.S. population identified by the Pew Forum's *2008 U.S. Religious Landscape*.)

asynchronous: stored, time-delayed

atheist: A person who rejects belief in deities, gods, or a God. (These people make up 1.6 percent of the U.S. population identified by the Pew Forum's *2008 U.S. Religious Landscape*.)

baptismal covenant: A promise made to God during the service of Holy Baptism that outlines how we strive to live our lives as Christians (specifically used in The Episcopal Church, Church of Latter Day Saints, and United Methodist Church).

blog: Short for weblog, a web-based collection of journal-like entries listed with the most recent on top. Most include text, audio, and video clips (sometimes called *vlogs*). Blogging sites include Blogger, TypePad, and WordPress.

charism: A word used in Christian theology, often by religious communities, to describe their spiritual orientation and any special characteristics of their mission or values that might be exhibited in communal life.

chat: Software imbedded in a website that enables two or more people to discuss topics live by typing words and phrases to each other. This is similar to instant messaging (IM), which is generally limited to communication between two people.

codes: Rules that govern everyday behavior and establish a community's moral, ethical, and behavioral expectations which range from complex systems of laws to unwritten customs and general ethical ideas.

collection: A religious community's self-defining oral and written texts and traditions.

computer-mediated communication (CMC): Communication that occurs by using two or more networked computers (i.e., chat rooms, e-mail, instant messages, web conferencing, virtual reality).

creeds: Explanations about the meaning or meanings of human life in the universe, which might be systematic theologies, oral traditions, narratives, and so forth.

cultuses: Multi-sensory rituals, gestures, signs, and symbols that orient a community to God and express the understandings and insights of the creeds and codes.

digital age (also called the information age or computer age): Current era of human history characterized by computer technology. Most recognized for an ability to manipulate voice, video, and data and, when networked, to send files to anyone, anywhere, anytime.

digital immigrant: Those born in the era of rotary telephones and manual typewriters.

digital native: Those who have always had desktop and palm-sized computers.

ecology of faith: The constellation of communal elements that converge to shape one's religious beliefs, attitudes, and practices. Within a Christian context, it recognizes the role of prayer and worship, teaching and learning, guidance and healing, service and outreach, enablement and advocacy, as well as less recognizable elements like place or space, generational perspectives, personal commitment, corporate intentionality, talking across difference, and relational openness. This combination of individual and communal elements invite, inform, and cultivate faithful members as well as form and transform individual and communal lives.

faith community: A group of people who are bound together by collected stories, creeds, and traditions including behavioral codes and cultus or rituals that express beliefs. These might be formal or informal. They could take the form of ethnic or cultural groups or formal institutions such as churches, denominations, etc.

(faith) formation: A lifelong, holistic and multi-modal process in which people deeply encounter a tradition to learn that tradition and respond to what they have experienced. The process includes individual and communal: hearing the tradition's stories, critically exploring and studying its texts and creeds, ritually reflecting on them (meditation, prayer, worship), and responding through behaviors that reflect the traditions and its ethical norms.

free or sustaining network time: The classification of radio and television programs in the United States that did not have commercial sponsorship or advertising. Free and sustained programs have been replaced by commercially sponsored programs today.

keystone species: A presence crucial to a community's survival that both orients and directs life in an ecosystem to participate in God's mission.

"making Christians": I use this phrase both to ground faith formation activity in Jesus' Great Commission and to highlight the intentionality it requires of faith communities and pastoral leaders. My goal is to encourage faith communities and pastoral leaders to create fertile ground—multi-sensory, multi-modal, interactive, and relationship-building places and spaces—within which seekers and members hear stories of faith, consider what they mean in relation to their own life stories, and decide how to respond. I do not mean to imply any form of indoctrination or institutional control.

member: A person belonging to a congregation and/or denomination. According to the Association of Religion Data Archives *Religious Congregations and Membership Study,* 2000, "members" are defined as "All individuals in a religious group with full membership status." Rules concerning membership vary by religious tradition. There may be confessions, behaviors, rituals, or other requirements for becoming a full member. Sometimes people use the word "member" as "adherent" to mean that they simply attend a congregation, whether or not they are full members of the congregation or denomination.

method: Refers to the type of engagement and interaction needed and/or desired as part of a communications effort. As implied by the discussion of broadcast/interactive, synchronous/asynchronous, and secure/open, methodologies can encourage or restrict interaction, demand attention at specific times or allow participants to make timing decisions, and encourage an individual or community's passive or active involvement as a message is proclaimed and embodied.

nones: Those who do not identify with any religion. (According to the October 2012 Pew Research Center's *Forum on Religion and Public Life,* 20 percent of the U.S. population identify as "nones.")

open source software: Publicly available software that may be able to be copied or modified without license or payment. Linux is an operating system developed by a group of software designers to replace operating systems like Microsoft Windows. Other open source software includes web browser Mozilla Firefox, course management Moosel, Microsoft Office competitor OpenOffice, and Google Docs.

podcast: An audio recording that can be listened to online or downloaded to one's computer, iPod, or other mp3 (a type of audio file) player.

religious literacy: According to Harvard Divinity School professor Diane Moore, a religiously literate person will possess 1) a basic understanding of the history, central texts (where applicable), beliefs, practices, and contemporary manifestations of several of the world's religious traditions as they arose out of and continue to be shaped by particular social, historical, and cultural contexts; and 2) the ability to discern and explore the religious dimensions of political, social, and cultural expressions across time and place.

rich media: A broad range of digital media—animation, sound, video, and/or interactivity—that may be embedded in a webpage, part of a mobile application, or downloaded for personal use. Rich media are often combined and used in emails, streaming media, Flash, and with programming languages such as Java, Javascript, and DHTML.

social networking: A method of connecting people using a collection of Internet-based tools for synchronous (at the same time) and asynchronous (time-delayed) interaction. For example, Facebook is a social networking site that enables individuals to post information about themselves, leave comments on a "wall" or bulletin board for anyone to see, interact live using chat, upload pictures, and create photo albums. Some social networking sites link people with similar interests. For example, LinkedIn and Plaxo are used for developing business contacts; Facebook and MySpace are more typically used for social interaction.

story-keeping, story-sharing, story-making: Story-keeping occurs as faithful people collect and maintain the wisdom of their tradition. This action defines and orients a community's beliefs and actions. Story-sharing requires interaction between story-keepers who understand the Christian vision of life with God as well as between those who know the stories of faith and those who do not. When defined by The Way, these countercultural actions both form disciples and invite others into discipleship.

Story-making moves faith into practice. By practicing faith, new members and longtime adherents are informed about, formed in, and transformed by God's presence; they also add to the Christian story, keeping it fresh and alive.

sustained critical interaction (SCI): Literally sustained (ongoing, regular), critical (deeply considered, analyzed, critiqued), interaction (engagement, genuine dialogue) between people and resources. It may be condensed with frequent interaction (i.e., one to three times a day for two weeks), less condensed with moderate interaction (one to three times per week for six weeks), or extended with less frequent interaction (i.e., one to three times per month for six months). Groups may meet on-site (physically together), online, or in some combination of on-site and online (hybrid or blended). Their interaction designed and facilitated as a space for intimate interpersonal communications can enable small groups to capitalize their social presence to deeply engage meaningful topics that can produce life-forming and transforming results.

synchronous: At the same time.

threaded discussion (sometimes called **discussion groups** or **bulletin boards**): One of the earliest forms of social networking, software is embedded in a website so that two or more people can have an asynchronous conversation by typing and leaving messages in a space that others can respond to at a later time. It is called "threaded" because conversations are typically organized by topic or thread. Some blogs invite reader comment and so blend into threaded discussions.

transformation: A re-orientation or re-creation of self and community that can take place as new insights and understandings are embraced.

Twitter: An application that sends a short text message called a **tweet** (140 characters or less).

vodcast/video podcast: Video recording offered the same way as a podcast. YouTube is a popular site for watching videos online.

web conference *or* **webinar:** A live, synchronous conference where participants can see, hear, and interact with each other. (Web conference tends to be more interactive and webinar tends to be more broadcast.) Audio may be offered over the Internet (**VOIP**—voice over Internet protocol) or by telephone. Adobe Connect, Skype, WebEx, and Wimba are some of the products that allow two or more people to conference online.

website: A static site (typically) that displays text, audio, and/or video information via the Internet.

wiki: Community publishing tool that allows multiple people to create an asynchronous website. Typically text based, it may be limited to a specific set of authors or open to the public so anyone can add information.

Ready to Operate Outside the Box?

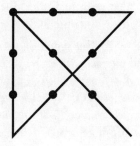